# PASTOR
# TO
# PASTOR

REVISED AND EXPANDED

# PASTOR TO PASTOR

## Tackling the Problems of Ministry

## Erwin Lutzer

Kregel
*Academic & Professional*

*Pastor to Pastor: Tackling the Problems of Ministry*

Copyright © 1998 by Erwin Lutzer

Published in 1998 by Kregel Publications, a division of Kregel, Inc., P.O. Box 2607, Grand Rapids, MI 49501.

**Library of Congress Cataloging-in-Publication Data**
Lutzer, Erwin W.
Pastor to Pastor: tackling the problems of ministry/ Erwin W. Lutzer.—Rev. and expanded.
     p.  cm.
Includes bibliographical references.
1. Clergy—Office. 2. Pastoral theology. I. Title.
BV660.2.L86  1998
253—dc21                                                    97-41096
                                                                   CIP
ISBN 978-0-8254-2947-7

Printed in the United States of America
2  3  4  5 / 12  11  10  09  08

# Contents

# Foreword

Numerous books are available to guide us as we face and solve personal and church problems. I have read many of those books and have found them helpful in one way or another.

Then, why another one?

Because this one aims for a much higher goal than simply the answering of questions or the solving of problems.

Personal spiritual growth: that is Erwin Lutzer's great concern as he shares these insights with you. The goal is not just the solving of church problems, as important as that is, but the spiritual development of both minister and congregation. After all, each problem we encounter is an opportunity for both pastor and people to face the situation honestly, seek God's wisdom diligently, and obey His will trustingly. The result? Spiritual growth all around!

Something else makes these chapters unique: they come from the heart and mind of a man who is a pastor, theologian, teacher, and philosopher, a man who has a heart for revival and renewal in the church. Erwin Lutzer draws from a wealth of learning that has been filtered through the grid of personal experience. No ivory tower ideas here, and no pious evasions!

Don't speed-read this book. Pause, ponder, pray, and grow!

Warren W. Wiersbe

# • 1 •

# The Call to the Ministry

## *Do We Need One?*

Suppose Charles Spurgeon and Billy Graham had chosen careers other than preaching. Would it have been all the same to God?

I don't think so. Though the idea is not popular today, I believe God still calls individuals to specific ministries, particularly preaching and teaching His Word.

During the past twenty years, missionaries have been telling us that there is no need for a specific call. Christ commanded us to preach the gospel; so, if we qualify, we should go. We shouldn't waste time waiting for a signal from heaven.

In *Decision Making and the Will of God*, Garry Friesen teaches that God has a sovereign will (His overall plan) and a moral will (His guidelines for life and belief) but no individual plan for every believer that we must "find."[1]

He asks us to remember how difficult it was to "find the will of God" when we had to make a particular decision and explains why that happened: we were looking for something that did not exist. We were seeking for a form of guidance that God did not promise to give.

Friesen exhorts us to make decisions on the basis of wisdom. We should gather all the information we can, weigh the pros and cons, and make our own decisions in faith. Of course, an important part of this is to consult with those who know us and to seek the insight of others.

He then asks about all the men called by God in the Scriptures. Because God spoke audibly to them, they had no doubt as to His will for them. God told Jeremiah directly that he was chosen for a specific ministry (Jer. 1:9–10). But God doesn't do that today, so those examples don't apply. We're expected to be obedient to God's moral will, but after that the decisions are ours. Any one of a number of choices would be fine with God.

There's some truth in that. Many of us grew up thinking we had to pry into the secret counsels of God whenever we had a decision to make. We tried to read His diary, but the print seemed blurred. His will was a mystery wrapped in an enigma. Doubtless we should have just gone ahead and made a reasonable decision. As one pastor told a friend, "Get a pure heart, and then do as you please."

We also believed that being called to the ministry required a Damascus-road experience. Short of that, we felt obligated to choose a "secular" vocation. I can remember many young men in Bible college and seminary discussing whether they were "called." Many of them hoped they were called but they weren't sure.

Furthermore, emphasizing a call to the ministry tends to exaggerate the distinction between clergy and laity. Every believer is a minister of God. To say that some Christians are called to specific ministries while others aren't seems contrary to the biblical teaching that each member of the body of Christ is important.

Friesen's position would also explain why some people have felt called to ministries for which they were ill-suited. Put simply, they were mistaken. What they thought was the Holy Spirit's leading was nothing but a personal hunch. You may have heard about the man who was called to preach; unfortunately, no one was called to listen!

One man, burned out at age forty, concluded that he had never been called to the ministry; he entered the ministry only to satisfy his mother. As a youngster he showed great promise in public speaking and church ministry, so she encouraged him to become a pastor. Now he concludes that was a mistake.

Despite the fact that we don't know as much about the "call" as we would like, I still believe that God gives a call to some people that is more than just a general call given to all believers. There is a call that is more than simply being gifted for ministry and even more than just a desire to preach or teach. Charles Bridges has a point when he says that ministerial failure can sometimes be traced "to the very threshold of the entrance to the work."

The late J. Oswald Sanders was right when he wrote, "The supernatural nature of the church demands a leadership that rises above the human. The overriding need of the church, if it is to discharge its obligation to the rising generation, is for leadership that is authoritative, spiritual and sacrificial."[2] Spurgeon, Graham, and hundreds of other preachers have said that they chose the ministry only because God chose them for it. Apparently Timothy didn't have an audible call. Yet I can't imagine Paul telling him that he could leave the ministry if he wished without also leaving the will of God. On the contrary, Paul urged him to fulfill his ministry. And when Timothy began to wonder about his call, Paul urged, "And for this reason I remind you to kindle afresh the gift of God which is in you through the laying on of my hands" (2 Tim. 1:6 NASB).

I don't see how anyone could survive in the ministry if he felt it was just his own choice. Some ministers scarcely have two good days back to back. They are sustained by the knowledge that God has placed them where they are. Ministers without such a conviction often lack courage and carry their resignation letter in their coat pocket. At the slightest hint of difficulty, they're gone.

I'm disturbed by those who preach and teach without a sense of calling. Those who consider the ministry to be one choice among many tend to have horizontal vision. They lack the urgency of Paul, who said, "Necessity is laid upon me." John Jowett says, "If we lose the sense of wonder of our commission, we shall become like common traders in a common market, babbling about common wares."[3]

Since God called numerous individuals to specific ministries in Bible times, it is only reasonable that He would do so today. Though He doesn't call audibly now that the New Testament is complete, we have an adequate basis by which to test the inner guidance of the Spirit.

## Characteristics of the Call

Let me risk my own definition of a call. *God's call is an inner conviction given by the Holy Spirit and confirmed by the Word of God and the body of Christ.*

Notice the three parts to the definition. First, it is an inner conviction. Feelings and hunches come and go. They may be based on impressions we had as children when we romanticized the idea of becoming a missionary. Or maybe we idolized the role of a pastor.

But a God-given compulsion is not deterred by obstacles. It gives us the single-mindedness needed for effective ministry. Some of us have had this conviction from our youth; others had a growing sense of urgency as they have studied the Bible; and still others perhaps had a less distinct but no less sure sense of direction. But the bottom line is the same: a strong desire to preach, join a mission team, or perhaps train others in the Word.

Of course, we don't all have to be called the same way. Circumstances and temperaments vary. I've already mentioned that for some people this conviction may be sudden; for others, it may be gradual. A person may sense no call at all until he is encouraged by discerning members of the body of Christ. Yet, despite those differences, there is a sense of purpose. Yes, "Woe is unto me, if I preach not the gospel!" (1 Cor. 9:16 KJV).

Second, the Word of God must confirm our call. We have to ask whether a person has the qualifications listed in 1 Timothy 3. Is he mature? Does he have the necessary gifts? Has he labored in the Word of God and in doctrine? Or might he have disqualified himself through moral or doctrinal compromise? Character is not all that is necessary, but it is the basic indispensable ingredient.

No doubt mistakes have been made when the scriptural qualifications have been overlooked in deference to a call. For a man to say that he's called is for some people reason enough to thrust him into ministry. But the church should not be hasty in ordaining those who are deemed called to such work. Though some people might have such a compulsion, they might have disqualified themselves, or their own perception might be mistaken.

On the other hand, churches have sometimes erred by refusing to ordain a man whom they deemed unfit for ministry. Perhaps the expected gifts were not present; perhaps the candidate did not appear to have the determination needed for ministry. And yet, as time went by, the man might have distinguished himself as a faithful minister. Even with the best of intentions we fail. But as was already mentioned, character must always be at the center of any evaluation of a call.

Certainly the qualifications of 1 Timothy 3 are more descriptive of the man's present character than his past character. But often his past, particularly since his conversion, is also relevant. If the man fails the test of the Scriptures, he must be excluded from ministry. Perhaps at a later time his call can be realized in another way. Third, the body of Christ helps us understand where we fit within the local church framework. The leaders of the church in Antioch were ministering to the Lord and fasting when the Holy Spirit said, "Set apart for Me Barnabas and Saul for the work to which I have called them" (Acts 13:2 NASB). The body enables its members to find their spiritual gifts and is a testing ground for further ministry. Those who are faithful in the least may later be entrusted with greater responsibility.

God might choose to confirm the call by special coincidental happenings or human mediation. I think of John Calvin's spending the night in Geneva when the fiery preacher Farrel pointed his finger at the young scholar and said, "If you do not stay here in Geneva and help the reform movement, God will curse you!" Unusual, I'd say, but would anyone disagree that Calvin was called of God to minister in Geneva? This incident was, of course, properly speaking, God's leading to a specific geographical location, but let us never limit the means God might use to get our attention and help us understand that His hand is upon us for special service.

My own call to ministry was confirmed when my pastor asked me to preach occasionally when I was in Bible school. The affirmation I received resonated with what I believed to be the leading of the Spirit within my heart and mind. I felt "called" as a child to preach, but if the body of Christ had not confirmed my conviction, I could not have pursued the ministerial path.

Often a person senses a call to the ministry but has no leading to a particular organization or church. Again, God uses the body of Christ or a mission board to clarify the next step. Often we are unaware of God's leading, but looking back we can see His hand of guidance on our lives. Indeed, some people who were initially unsure of their call have nevertheless done an effective work for God.

Though the details are different in each case, the end result must be the same: a sense of the divine initiative, a commission that leaves a man or a woman with a settled assurance that he or she is doing what God desires.

## Our Response to the Call

Our response to God's call should be one of amazed humility. Each of us should have a sense of authority and boldness. We should be characterized by unusual earnestness and diligence in study and prayer. Jowett perhaps overstated it only slightly when he wrote, "The call of the Eternal must ring through the rooms of his soul as clearly as the sound of the morning-bell rings through the valleys of Switzerland, calling the peasants to early prayer and praise."[4] Spurgeon discouraged men from entering the ministry. He told them plainly that if they could take another vocation they should. He wanted in the ministry only those who felt strongly that they had no other alternative. Luther warned that one should flee the ministry, even if he were wiser than Solomon and David, unless one was called. And "if God needs thee, He will know how to call thee."

How do I account for those who have dropped out of the ministry? Should they feel as if they have failed in their calling? It's possible of course, that some of them have failed. But that doesn't mean God can't use them in other vocations, for He is always working in spite of our failures. Many fallen pastors can be restored as brothers, but they have disqualified themselves from spiritual leadership. Others simply might have considered the ministry as one opportunity among many and therefore lacked the passion that would make them deeply committed to God.

But there may be other explanations. Perhaps such ministers were called, but the body of Christ failed them. Young men have been ruined by critical congregations.

Others may not have failed at all, but worldly standards of success would interpret their ministry that way. Isaiah had a marvelous call, but from a human perspective, he failed in the ministry. Indeed, God told him that practically no one would listen to what he had to say.

Then again, some ministers may be like John Mark; discouraged, they give up at first, but they may become effective in a later ministry.

We do not know all of the contingencies, but let us not allow those difficulties to rob us of a divine sense of calling that gives us our courage and authority. And, as the old saying goes, "If God calls us to preach, let us not stoop to become a king."

## • 2 •

# A Congregation's Expectations

## *Can We Adjust?*

"If you have the reputation of being an early riser, you can sleep until noon."

I don't remember where I read this bit of insight, but it reminded me that a congregation's perception of its pastor influences, for good or for ill, the effectiveness of his ministry. If he's perceived as dishonest, inept, or indiscreet, his words and actions will be interpreted through a negative grid. If he's thought of as godly and competent, he will be given the benefit of the doubt even when he fails.

Often, this situation puts him at a disadvantage. If he should lose the congregation's goodwill, his ministry might soon be over. But if he consciously attempts to establish and maintain a correct impression, he courts spiritual disaster. We all stand in need of perspective in this matter.

### The Pressures of Public Ministry

Pastors are continually open to public evaluation. Preach nine good messages and one blooper, and some people will remember only the message that bombed. Walk past a deacon without acknowledging him, and you might rankle his feelings. And if a disgruntled church member begins some gossip, a little leaven could leaven the whole lump.

We're also under pressure because few members of the congregation know the demands of our schedules. One pastor asked his deacons to outline how they thought he spent his time. Although he was working a seventy-hour week, they had difficulty coming up with a forty-hour week. We've all laughed at the child who says to the pastor's kid, "My dad isn't like yours—he works for a living." But it hurts just the same.

Once you've gained a reputation, you're more or less stuck with it. I read about a pastor who was at a baseball game when a church member needed him. The irate parishioner spread the story that the pastor spent all his time at the ballpark. Although the pastor nearly ruined his health and family working overtime to correct the false impression, it lingered.

Such perceptions, whether true or false, can wield awesome authority over us. If we are self-conscious, always wondering how well we are liked, we'll soon be slaves to the pulse of our popularity. We will do everything with an eye on our ratings.

At that point, we'll lose our authority to minister. "The fear of man brings a snare" (Prov. 29:25 NASB). We'll desire to remain neutral in disputes, trying earnestly to agree with everyone. We will not administer church discipline for fear of criticism. We'll back away from any unpopular stand, even when it's right. Many pastors are intimidated by confrontation.

I'm not saying we should be insensitive. We've all met the pastor who takes pride in "not caring what anyone thinks" and callously disregards the feelings of others. I'm talking about a lack of boldness even in matters that are clear in the Scriptures.

We'll also find it difficult to rejoice in the success of other pastors. Television has brought the superchurch to our parishioners' living rooms. Comparison is inevitable. We've all had to chime in enthusiastically when we heard glowing comments about the great blessing that "so and so" has been to the life of one of our members. We want to rejoice, too, but the joy doesn't come easily. We may even take secret delight in another's failure. One assistant pastor, who was an apparent threat to the senior pastor, told me, "Nothing would delight him more than if I were to blow it."

When we're overly sensitive to what others think, we'll also live with guilt—the nagging feeling that we could be doing more. Since by definition our work is never finished, we then carry it home with us. My wife would tell you that sometimes I'm not at home even when I'm physically present. I'm preoccupied with the pressures of the day and the ones I'll face tomorrow.

In the process, our faith is eroded. Christ directed this question to the Pharisees: "How can you believe, when you receive glory from one another, and you do not seek the glory that is from the one and only God?" (John 5:44 NASB). The desire for human praise and the faith to minister cancel each other—seek the one and the other eludes you.

When in conflict with the Pharisees, who were somewhat less than enthusiastic about His ministry, Jesus said, "And He who sent Me is with Me; He has not left Me alone, for I always do the things that are pleasing to Him" (John 8:29 NASB).

How can we be that free, that single-minded?

## Freedom to Serve

Our Lord was free from men's opinions about Him. Though He cared what they thought because He knew that their eternal destiny depended on whether they believed in Him, His actions were never calculated to gain their praise. The will of the Father was all that mattered. And if the Father was pleased, the Son was pleased. That was why He was just as content when washing the disciples feet as He was when preaching the Sermon on the Mount.

I've known pastors who were like that—surrendered, secure, and free from actions motivated by a desire for human praise. They felt no need to prove themselves or be in the limelight. No grudging admissions about other people's successes—just freedom and joy in the work of the Lord.

What characteristics could we expect if we were brought to such a place of surrender?

First, we would not let people push us into their mold. We all live with the tension between what we are and what others want us to be. We'd like to fulfill the exalted expectations that many people have for us, but we can't. If we know ourselves realistically, both our strengths and weaknesses, we'll not think that we are God's gift to every human need.

Christ faced this tension, too. After He fed the multitude, the crowd sought to crown Him king. But He went off by Himself, refusing to consider the offer, even though He knew that this was a disappointment to His followers. His miracles generated expectations He simply could not fulfill at the time.

Yet before His death He could say He had finished the Father's work, though hundreds of people were still sick and thousands more had not believed on Him. But the pressure of those needs did not blur His vision to please only the Father.

The more blessed people are by our ministry, the greater their expectations of us will be. If we let them, they will lead us to believe that we're the only ones who can lead people to Christ, counsel the emotionally troubled, or visit in the hospital. We do well to heed the words of Bunyan: "He that is low need fear no fall."

And if we believe that we are God's answer to every need, we'll also accept every invitation for lunch, attend all committee meetings, and take outside speaking engagements when asked—all at the expense of our families, our health, and, most of all, our relationship with God.

Let's not let our successes propel us into a role that is beyond our strengths and abilities. Our self-image must always be adjusted to fit reality. Saying no graciously is an essential characteristic of a man who has submitted his will to God.

Second, we would profit from criticism. No one likes criticism, particularly when it's unfair. Furthermore, we usually don't get a chance to give our side of the story without risking additional misunderstanding. Yet sometimes, even when the criticism is valid, our pride prevents us from learning from the experience. When we think of ourselves more highly than we ought to think, we may believe we are beyond rebuke.

Paul also received criticism. He was under fire for going to the Gentiles and was imprisoned because he refused to compromise the inclusive claim of the gospel. Sometimes the condemnation was personal and vindictive: "His letters are weighty and strong, but his personal presence is unimpressive, and his speech contemptible" (2 Cor. 10:10 NASB). But he was undeterred. He knew that God would vindicate him.

Every leader has his critics. If we are especially sensitive, if we cannot tolerate differences of opinion, and if we refuse to learn from criticism, we're still clinging to our reputations.

Many lies were published about revivalist George Whitefield to discourage the crowds from hearing him, but he responded by saying that he could wait until God rendered the final judgment. Such a man of faith cannot be destroyed.

Third, we would not be afraid to let our humanity show. Our congregations believe that we are different—free from the emotional and spiritual struggles of others. After all, if we are not walking in uninterrupted victory, who is left to lean on? Heroes are in short supply, and a pastor who has been a blessing to his flock is a good candidate to fulfill the role.

If we refuse to talk about our failures and share only our victories, we'll reinforce that distorted perception. Eventually, it will give way to myth. One pastor confessed in exhaustion, "My congregation expects me to be perfect." I suggested to him that he be willing to help his people "demythologize" him by discretely letting at least a few of his faults show.

Our lack of authenticity creates a burden that is too heavy to bear. Struggling under its weight, we'll assume we have, indeed, arrived spiritually and, hence, be blind to our shortcomings or kill ourselves trying to live up to others' expectations. We'll also tend to withdraw, fearful that people will get to know what we're really like.

Yet what pastor hasn't done some things of which he's ashamed? If our congregations could open our minds for inspection, we'd all resign in shame and disgrace. We can help our people better when we let them know that we stand with them in the quest for righteousness, neither above nor off to the side, where the arrows of Satan and the passions of the flesh can't touch us. Honesty communicates much better than a false sense of perfection.

One church member wrote a letter to his pastor asking in part, "Are you as human as we are? Have you struggled with some of the same problems we face during the week? Is there discord in your home? Heartache? Anguish? Won't you share that with us, too, as you share your doctrine, your theology, your exposition?"

Finally, we would not see the success of another as a threat to our own ministry. When the Holy Spirit came upon the seventy elders during the ministry of Moses, two men continued to prophesy. Joshua, jealous for Moses' reputation, suggested that Moses restrain them. But Moses replied, "Are you jealous for my sake? Would that all the Lord's people were prophets, that the Lord would put His Spirit upon them!" (Num. 11:29 NASB).

Here was a man who could rejoice in the success of others. He did not want to keep his gift to himself, nor did he have to defend his call to the ministry. Many pastors struggle over the success of another, especially if that individual is on their staff. The fact that God sometimes uses those who are less gifted, or even less authentic than we would like, brings the sin of envy to the surface.

But the person who has died to himself will bow humbly, resisting the temptation to envy simply because God is generous. In the parable of the workers in the vineyard, the landowner said to those who had worked longer hours and grumbled about equal pay, "Is it not lawful for me to do what I wish with what is my own? Or is your eye envious because I am generous?" (Matt. 20:15 NASB).

It's God's prerogative to bless some people more than we think He should. Apart from such grace, we'd all be lost. Friends of John the Baptist were concerned because some of his disciples were leaving to follow Christ. John responded, "A man can receive nothing, unless it has been given him from heaven" (John 3:27 NASB).

If we believed those words, we'd be free from all comparisons, competition, and self-consciousness in the ministry. We'd serve with a glad heart, accepting our role.

Later, John added, "He must increase, but I must decrease" (v. 30).

Even if our ministry should be diminished, we can accept it more easily if Christ is honored through submission to His will. Since our ministry is God-given, we can neither take credit for it nor insist that it continue.

If we have become men pleasers, let's repent. Such an attitude is an affront to God. Subtly, we are preaching ourselves, not Christ.

If you have the reputation of being an early riser, you can sleep until noon. But God knows when you get out of bed, and His perception is the one that really counts.

# • 3 •

## Surviving a Skirmish

### *How Should We Relate to the Board?*

Perhaps the most sensitive pressure point in a church organization is the relationship between the pastor and the church board. The details differ, but the story is the same: the pastor wants to take the church one direction, and the board wants to take it another. The pastor believes he receives his orders from God, so the board had better follow him. But the board is unconvinced and digs in its heels, settling down for a long power struggle.

Division can come over anything from the building program to the order of the morning worship service. Pastors and boards have parted company over whether wine should be served for Communion, divorced people should teach in Sunday school, or the carpet should be blue or red.

The issue is often irrelevant; it's who wins that counts. What's at stake is power, and the question of who's in charge must be settled. Eventually, the issue will be settled but often at the expense of a split.

As pastors, we sometimes bring division on ourselves. For some pastors, submitting to the board is a sign of weakness, a denial of a God-given mandate. Some of us think that to be called of God is a guarantee that we know God's will for our congregations. Furthermore, we may think that God blesses only those pastors who stand up for their views regardless of the cost. Our desire to vindicate ourselves is powerful. If our egos are not subdued by the cross, we'll even be tempted to misuse Scripture, warning our detractors that they had better not "touch the Lord's anointed."

The more dictatorial the pastor, the more necessary it will be for him to win on every issue. He interprets even minor matters as a referendum on his leadership, so he must get his way every time. And if the board doesn't grant his wish, he'll resort to pressure, by-passing the board to appeal to the congregation or coercing other leaders in the church. Or he will write an unauthorized letter to the congregation in defense of himself, often in the interest of truth, for the sake of "setting the record straight." Unfortunately, few pastors today are willing to leave some disputes for the Lord to set right at the judgment seat. Such a pastor may not realize that what he gains in the power struggle he loses in credibility and respect.

Peter had a different understanding of the elder's role: "Shepherd the flock of God among you, not under compulsion, but voluntarily, according to the will of God; and not for sordid gain, but with eager-ness; nor yet as lording it over those allotted to your charge, but proving to be examples to the flock" (1 Peter 5:2–3 NASB).

Christ taught that the primary quality of leadership was servanthood, not a dictatorial spirit. The Gentiles sought superiority and control; believers should seek humility and submission. The only clear instance of one-man rule in the New Testament is that of Diotrephes, who loved to have the preeminence (3 John 9).

I'm not suggesting, however, that the board is always innocent. I've heard many horror stories of church boards that have driven their pastors to unnecessary resignations. But I'd like to suggest some basic principles that can help us in negotiating the inevitable differ-ences that arise.

## The Principle of Accountability

Everyone on the board (including the pastor) must be subject to the board's consensus. After having conducted an exhaustive study of every relevant New Testament passage on the topic, Bruce Stabbert states in his book *The Team Concept,* "In all these passages, there is not one passage which describes a church being governed by one pastor."[1]

Of course, in Baptist polity, deacons usually assume the responsi-bilities that elders held in the New Testament. But the principle of plurality of leadership still applies, regardless of how churches are organized. The pastor, therefore, has no authority to act independently of his board. He cannot override its vote by an appeal to his divine call simply because all the elders have equal authority. They, too, have a divine call, albeit to a different role and responsibility. Nor should the pastor threaten to resign unless the controversy merits his resignation. More than one board has called a pastor's bluff and forced him to eat his words or follow through with his threat. But what if the board is obviously wrong? If the matter involves eternal truth, such as important doctrinal or moral issues, the pastor must warn the offending party of the consequences. There are times when a split may be necessary. As the apostle Paul taught, "For there must also be factions among you, in order that those who are approved may have become evident among you" (1 Cor. 11:19 NASB).

But I've seldom heard of a split because of doctrinal or moral error. Usually it's because of the building program, the pastor's leadership style, or floundering church programs.

When difficulties arise, the pastor often feels slighted, unappreciated, and misunderstood. The innate desire we all have to justify ourselves may take over, and the pastor determines that he will not leave until justice is done.

Paul, however, admonishes us not to avenge ourselves but to let God settle our accounts. Blessed is the pastor-elder who can accept wrong without compromise but also without retaliation. To clarify a matter is one thing, but to persist in being defensive is quite another.

However much he may try to convince the board of his viewpoint, the bottom line is that he must submit to its authority unless a clear point of Scripture is at stake. It's better to leave than to stay to prove a point or to get "justice."

## Leadership Through the Board

The pastor must share his vision with those to whom he is accountable. In this task, time and patience bring fruitful dividends when the board acts as one in making decisions for the benefit of the body.

But that kind of unity comes only through prayer and hard work. If the previous pastor had a tarnished reputation, the board will need time to develop confidence in the new pastor's integrity. There will be a trial period until mutual confidence is established.

When a group decision is made, there is also shared responsibility. Does that mean the pastor shouldn't be a strong leader? Not at all. Most boards expect their pastor to take the initiative, to give the ministry direction. In 1 Timothy 5:17, Paul writes, "Let the elders who rule well be considered worthy of double honor, especially those who work hard at preaching and teaching."

The New Testament allows for strong leadership within the plurality of elders. However, if the pastor dictates to the board, and it is not an integral part of the decision-making process, its members may eventually polarize against him. A board may have diversity of opinion about a proposal, of course. But the pastor and the board must be willing to pray and wait until a consensus emerges.

A word of caution: Sometimes a board doesn't stand behind its decisions if members voted yes just for the sake of pleasing the pastor or for the sake of unity. I know one instance in which the board voted unanimously to ask for a staff member's resignation, but individual members reversed themselves after going home and talking it over with their wives. The ability to sense whether a board is sold on an idea or just going along for the ride is an art.

## The Board's Responsibility to the Board

The board must keep its members from becoming unruly. The following scenario has happened a thousand times. One board member, usually the unofficial "church boss," itches for recognition and control. He begins to oppose the pastor and pretends to speak for others. The other board members are intimidated. After all, they reason, he's been in the church for years, and his wife plays the piano. So they sit by, hoping the problem will go away. But it only gets worse, and discord spreads.

In one church, an elder ruined the ministry of three pastors by using the same strategy. He would befriend the pastor in the first year and then turn against him in the second. Because of his influence, he'd generate enough opposition to force a showdown. The board was at a loss to deal with the problem, so the members let it go on.

Unfortunately, the board usually believes the pastor is expendable. Pastors come and go, but the elder stays forever. The board must have the strength to discipline its own members. If not, church leaders adopt a double standard, and the work of God is hindered.

Paul gives some specific instructions for confronting an elder. An accusation should not be received except on the basis of two or three witnesses, and if an elder continues in sin, he should be rebuked publicly (1 Tim. 5:19–20). The pastor must enlist the cooperation of other board members when calling a fellow elder to accountability.

If Satan can't get a pastor to ruin his own reputation, he will try to create friction between the pastor and the board. Without unity, we can conquer neither the world nor the devil. As Benjamin Franklin said at the signing of the Declaration of Independence, "We must all hang together, or assuredly, we shall all hang separately."

Let's redouble our effort to obey Paul's admonition to be "diligent to preserve the unity of the Spirit in the bond of peace" (Eph. 4:3). Anything less will cause the body of Christ to work against itself.

Let the hard work begin.

## • 4 •

# Problem People

---

## *Confrontation or Compromise?*

A friend of mine, fresh out of Bible college, became the pastor of a small country church. One day, the elders asked him to visit a wealthy member who hadn't been attending regularly but continued to contribute to the church coffers.

"We don't think he's even a Christian," they said. So at their insistence, he visited the old gentleman and asked him point-blank if he was saved. The man became incensed at the pastor's audacity to suggest that he, a self-made man, was not a Christian.

Several weeks later, the church building burned. The congregation met in a schoolroom to decide what to do. After they decided to rebuild, the man whose salvation had been questioned stood up.

"This young man had the nerve to question whether I was a Christian," he stated. "What do you suggest we do about it?"

He sat down with an air of importance, waiting for a response. Silence.

"I move we terminate him as pastor," the man said.

There was some discussion, but not one of the elders rose to defend their pastor and explain that he had been acting on their request. Later, a vote was taken, and the young man was given two weeks to resign.

After the meeting, no one came to speak to him except a school janitor who overheard what had happened over the public address system. The pastor left the building and began walking in blinding rain mile after mile, scarcely aware of where he was going.

That was thirty-five years ago. He has never pastored another church. He has served the Lord as a layperson, but that one devastating experience could never be erased from his memory.

## Techniques of Opposition

Most of us haven't had such an experience. But perhaps we've had board members who supported us in meetings but criticized us to others on Sunday. We've all had to work with people who are negative, critical, and obnoxious. In one church, a man takes notes diligently with the intent of keeping the pastor straight on his theology. After each service he confronts the pastor, explaining how he could improve his preaching.

Recently, a pastor told me about a parishioner who opposed his ministry. The critic would approach a member of the congregation and throw him some bait.

"You know, I've met people within the congregation who question whether the pastor should . . ."

If the person said he strongly supported the pastor, the man would back off. Because he claimed to be speaking for others in the congregation, he faced no personal risk. But if the person expressed some agreement, the critic would sow bitter seeds of discord. He was a garbage collector. He went from person to person gathering grievances. Eventually, he stirred up enough trouble to force the pastor's resignation.

Ironically, sometimes the person who befriends the pastor when he first arrives is the one who later turns against him. The man is attracted to the pastor because he wants to brief him on the way things really are. But if the pastor doesn't agree with him right down the line, he will soon become his adversary. To see the pastor succeed would be his greatest disappointment.

The problem person sees himself not as difficult to live with but as a loyal member of the congregation just doing his duty. Many such a person has sent a pastor to an early grave either unaware of his destructive influence or sincerely thinking that the pastor deserved to be punished. Remember, disgruntled people always cloak their actions with verses of Scripture; they speak of having the "pastor's best interests at heart." Spirituality and the Bible are both pressed into service to justify self-serving or unwise behavior.

This problem is difficult because most problem people will not face the pastor directly to resolve their disagreements. They ignore Christ's teaching about going directly to the person with whom one has a dispute (Matt. 18:15–17). They prefer to give their speech at a public meeting where they can claim to speak for others—and at the same time poison the atmosphere of the whole church. The pastor may find it difficult to defend himself for fear he might be viewed as unspiritual. And even if he does have a legitimate defense, the damage has been done.

One elder who was silent when the board voted to borrow money for a building program stood at a congregational meeting and insisted that the church was in sin because it had chosen to borrow money. The division that resulted took about a year to resolve. Of course, it never dawned on him that he was in sin for publicly chastising the church rather than voicing his concern in board meetings and working though proper channels of authority.

## Handling Dragons

How shall we cope with difficult people in our congregations? First, we must listen carefully to what they are saying—they might be right. Some pastors are so sensitive to criticism that they tend to reject all negative comments. But even if we think the person has been unfair, there may be some truth to what he has said.

Many a potential problem has been diffused by simply giving our friend an honest hearing. In fact, he may be doing us a favor. "Reprove a wise man, and he will love you" (Prov. 9:8 NASB). Others in the congregation may have the same criticisms but haven't felt free to tell you. In *Well-Intentioned Dragons*, Marshall Shelley writes, "Solitary shots should be ignored, but when they come from several directions, it's time to pay attention. As someone else once said, 'If one calls you a donkey, ignore him. If two call you a donkey, check for hoof prints. If three call you a donkey, get a saddle.'"[1]

After you've heard the friend's criticism, you must see the problem in perspective. You can receive a hundred compliments, but it's that one criticism that sticks in your mind. Many a pastor has spent a sleepless night because of a single negative remark.

But now is the time for sober analysis. Is the criticism at least partially correct? Is it because of a difference in style or leadership philosophy, or might it be a personality conflict? If you've hurt someone's feelings, even unintentionally, humble yourself and ask forgiveness. If you can resolve the difference by a personal meeting, by all means do it.

One pastor with an opposing board member sensed trouble for months, but he refused to take the man out for lunch because he feared direct confrontation. His refusal only increased the alienation. Finally, reconciliation became impossible.

Not all disagreements are necessarily bad or evidence of carnality. Remember, Barnabas wanted to take Mark on the second missionary journey, but Paul disagreed, reminding him that the young man had deserted them in Pamphylia. Luke wrote, "And there arose such a sharp disagreement that they separated from one another, and Barnabas took Mark with him and sailed away to Cyprus" (Acts 15:39 NASB).

Sometimes there is no easy answer to who is right or wrong. If possible, work out a solution to accommodate the critic's legitimate complaints. Maybe you could change the order of worship from time to time or begin to teach that Bible class. Many a potential trouble-maker has been diffused by reasonable compromise.

But there are some critics (Shelley calls them "dragons") who will never be satisfied. We've all had critics who criticized us (and everyone else) to satisfy their own deep personal problem; they might have ego needs that defy resolution. They are like the drunkard who'd had strong-smelling cheese smeared on his mustache before he left the saloon. As the man staggered into the clear night air he muttered, "The whole world stinks!"

With such a person, you must make a choice. Ask yourself, "How deeply do I feel about this matter? Can I live with the situation, accepting it from God as His means of personal refinement?" Spurgeon said, "Get a friend to tell you your faults, or better still, welcome an enemy who will watch you keenly and sting you savagely. What a blessing such an irritating critic will be to a wise man, what an intolerable nuisance to a fool!"[2]

## Taking a Stand

But perhaps you think the matter is important enough to put your reputation on the line. If there appears to be no resolution, and if the disagreement interferes with your ability to minister, then you must throw the matter into the lap of the board and be prepared to accept the consequences.

Scripture teaches that those who walk disorderly should be disciplined. Paul wrote, "And if anyone does not obey our instruction in this letter, take special note of that man and do not associate with him, so that he may be put to shame. And yet do not regard him as an enemy, but admonish him as a brother" (2 Thess. 3:14–15).

If the board backs you decisively and admonishes those who sow discord, you can continue your ministry with confidence. If you have built solid relationships with board members, they will be prepared to give your viewpoint due consideration. But if the board thinks the criticism is justified, or if the men are too weak to stand against those who would polarize the church, you may have no recourse but to resign. Seldom does the decision to "stay no matter what" have a good result.

Unfortunately, board members tend to side with those who've been their friends in the church for many years. It's particularly difficult when the troublemaker is married to the choir leader or is related to four other families in the congregation. Unfortunately, most of us cannot handle problems with complete objectivity; friendships, old loyalties, and partial information often cloud our ability to act as we should.

In one church, the entire board opposed the pastor because of the persuasive power of one woman who had indirectly controlled the church for years. In a vendetta against the pastor, she even suggested that he should divorce his wife, though they had been happily married for thirty-eight years! Yet, board members were so mesmerized by her that they accepted her criticisms, and the pastor was forced to resign.

In such situations, a pastor can either carry his hurts with him and poison his future usefulness to God or come to terms with the injustice. This particular pastor committed the matter to the Lord, believing that God would ultimately untangle the mess at the judgment seat. He has been blessed in special ways and will undoubtedly be used of God in the future.

Peter Marshall said, "It is a fact of Christian experience that life is a series of troughs and peaks. In His efforts to get permanent possession of the soul, God relies on the troughs more than the peaks.

And some of His special favorites have gone through longer and deeper troughs than anyone else."[3]

Remember, when we encounter dragons who are believers, God loves them too. He can use us in their lives, but He can also use them in ours. There is no one correct answer to all situations. But Shelley does state one cardinal rule: *When attacked by a dragon, do not become one.*

As my friend said, "God will have to untangle many things at the judgment seat." Sometimes it's best to leave the problem with Him rather than try to solve it ourselves.

# • 5 •

# Preaching

## *How Can We Reach Their Souls?*

Charles Spurgeon once walked into a new auditorium and tested the acoustics by shouting, "Behold the Lamb of God, which taketh away the sin of the world." A workman who overheard him was smitten with conviction and was converted.

Some preachers get a better response than others. If ten pastors preached the same message verbatim, the results would not be the same. Some pastors exude instant charisma; others are more yielded to the Spirit or have greater gifts. It's not just *what* is said but *who* says it that makes the difference.

Sermons with good content may fall flat for many reasons. Perhaps the most common reason is that they are delivered with an absence of feeling. We've all fallen into the rut of preaching unfelt truth. We've rattled through a message as if it were a stock market report at the end of a lackluster day of trading. Vance Havner said, "I've never heard a sermon from which I didn't get something, but I've had some mighty close calls."

When I was a teenager, I wondered why the pastor didn't simply mimeograph his messages and mail them. That would have enabled us to get the truth without the effort of going to church. Now I wonder if I entertained such thoughts because the pastor preached so nonchalantly that his personal delivery added little to the message.

Preaching is not just giving a message. "Is preaching the art of making a sermon and delivering it?" asked Bishop William A. Quayle. "Why no, that's not preaching. *Preaching is the art of making a preacher and delivering that!*"

It's the preacher's delivering himself that is absent from so many of our pulpits on Sunday mornings. Many preachers have no fire in their bones.

Michael Tucker, a pastor in Colorado, writes of an effective preacher: "Preaching must pump his heart until he lives and breathes the message. The message will hound him, drive him, even explode within him. So great will be the desire to preach that he will find it difficult to wait for the time to deliver the message of God."

George Whitefield preached with intensity. He wrote to a friend, "Speak every time as if it was your last. Weep out, if possible, every argument, and as it were, compel them to cry, 'Behold how he loveth us!'"

Jesuit theologian Walter Burghardt deplores the perfunctory remarks made by priests in their homilies. He laments that the laity of the Roman Catholic Church is "puzzled by our ability to declaim about the divine without a shred of feeling or emotion." His words apply to many evangelical ministers, too.

## Three Styles of Preaching

Richard Owen Roberts, author of the book *Revival*, speaks of three levels of sermon preparation. The first level is mouth-to-ear preaching. That's when a man is greatly concerned about the choice and organization of his words. He's conscious of the need for good illustrations and vivid descriptions. He's careful to work on key phrases and unique expressions. A typical listener responds, "What a lovely sermon. I really enjoyed it!"

Then there is head-to-head preaching. It stimulates thought and challenges the minds of the listeners. The preacher aims at being well organized, theologically accurate, and enlightening. At the door he hears, "That was a great sermon. I never thought of that before."

In soul-to-soul preaching, the preacher spends hours preparing his message but equal time preparing his soul. Only that kind of preaching results in conversions and personal holiness.

That explains why some of the most effective preachers are not the most eloquent. Some preachers who have only ordinary gifts are used in extraordinary ways because they deliver not only the message but also themselves. Quite literally, they become the message they are preaching.

## The Three Persons Participate in Preaching

How can we preach in such a way that we stir the emotions and move the will? Shouting won't do it, nor will dramatic stories. We must become intimately aware of the three personalities involved in the preaching event.

The first such personality is God. Peter wrote, "Whoever speaks, let him speak, as it were, the utterances of God" (1 Peter 4:11 NASB). A preacher speaks on God's behalf; if the sermon is boring, repetitious, or perfunctory, that's the way the congregation will perceive God's message.

Does God have a relevant word for today? Has He spoken with clarity about the issues that face the members of our congregations? Can He demolish walls of hatred and suspicion among families and believers? All of these and a hundred other questions are being answered when we speak on His behalf.

We can't represent Him effectively unless we spend time meditating on His attributes. We must stand in awe of His holiness as displayed in that thunderous revelation at Mount Sinai, of His sovereignty in creation and history, of His love as shown at the cross.

For thus says the high and exalted One
Who lives forever, whose name is Holy,
"I dwell on a high and holy place,
And also with the contrite and lowly of spirit
In order to revive the spirit of the lowly
And to revive the heart of the contrite."
(Isa. 57:15 NASB)

We must be diligent in rekindling our emotional fires for preaching by grasping anew the wonder of our privilege as messengers of the Most High. We must know Him well before we can effectively represent Him to others.

The second person invoked in the sermon is the listener. Let's discard the idea that if we talk others will listen. People do not come to church with open minds. Haddon Robinson, of Gordon Conwell School of Theology, says, "Heads are neither open nor hollow. Heads have lids, screwed on tightly, and no amount of pouring can force ideas inside. Minds open only when their owners sense a need to open them.

Even then, ideas must still filter through layers of experience, habit, prejudice, fear, and suspicion."

Anger, for example, may prevent a person from listening. A parishioner's teenage son fell asleep at the wheel of his car and was killed. The insensitive pastor said to the distraught father, "Don't expect me to take the funeral, because I'm going on vacation." The father told me later, "Even though he was a good preacher, after that remark I never heard a word he said in his sermons."

That anecdote illustrates an important principle of communication: You can preach up a storm, but if a person is not disposed to listen, it penetrates no farther than water on a marble slab.

Or maybe the parishioner is thinking about the pressures of the past week, family problems, or financial reversals. Add to that the depravity of the natural mind and Satan's ability to snatch the Word of God from people's hearts, and it's a miracle that communication takes place at all.

We can't pry through this grid unless we genuinely love our people and bear their needs close to our hearts. Information alone will not change their attitudes and behavior. They must see us bleed along with them. We must enter into the hurts of their world.

Finally, there is the preacher. He must apply the truth to himself before he shares it with others. That is difficult for those of us who preach two or three times a week. But we cannot afford to pass on truths that are supposed to work for others but haven't worked for us. We must share ourselves so that people can see we are a part of the message we are bringing. Our people want to know that we are human, that we share in the griefs and hopes of mortals.

Expressing honest feelings isn't easy. Bombarded with human need, we insulate ourselves from the emotional overload we encounter daily. We are unable to weep for those in need as Christ did when He stood on the Mount of Olives and wept for Jerusalem. Seminary has trained us to think deeply but not to feel deeply. One writer well says that "a preacher must think clearly and feel deeply and cause his hearers to do the same."

The effectiveness of our preaching would rise dramatically if we followed a simple rule: Let's not preach beyond our experience. When we share the message God has given us, we should know it well enough that we can concentrate on its content rather than worry about remembering its outline. Only then can we say with authority, "Thus says the Lord."

Perhaps we ought to follow John Owen, a Puritan scholar and pastor of the seventeenth century, in taking a vow before we step into the pulpit: "I therefore hold myself bound in conscience and in honor, not even to imagine that I have attained a proper knowledge of any one article of truth, much less to publish it, unless through the Holy Spirit I have had such a taste of it, in its spiritual sense, that I may be able from the heart to say with the psalmist, 'I have believed and therefore have spoken.'"[1]

When I taught homiletics at an evangelical seminary, I wanted to illustrate to the class how dependent we must be on God when preaching, especially to the unconverted. So I held the class in a cemetery and began by reading Ephesians 2:1–6, "And you were dead in your trespasses and sins. . . ." Then I asked one of the students to preach to one of the dead, telling a man who had long since been buried that the day of resurrection had come. When he refused (thinking that I wasn't serious), I did it myself. "Jonathan!" I shouted at the grave stone, "It is the day of resurrection!" Thankfully, there was no response!

Then I turned to the students and said, "I felt very foolish doing that. I knew that Jonathan, buried in 1912, would not rise. But that is how foolish we are when we preach the gospel, except for one fact: God might graciously grant a resurrection!"

Paul continues, "But God, being rich in mercy, because of His great love with which He loved us, even when we were dead in our transgressions, made us alive together with Christ (by grace you have been saved), and raised us up with Him, and seated us with Him in the heavenly places, in Christ Jesus" (Eph. 2:4–6 NASB).

I reminded the class that God asked Ezekiel to speak to dry bones, and God then created flesh and breathed life into the corpses. Then we knelt in the cemetery to ask God to give us the grace to preach the gospel with a sense of helplessness, with a conscious dependence on God and His grace. Only He can raise the dead; only He can grant them the ability and the faith to believe.

In brief, my philosophy of preaching is to expect people to be changed forever because of the ministry of the Word. Of course, that might not always be achieved, but if we aim at anything less, I fear we shall hit it! If we spend as much time preparing our hearts as we do our minds, our congregations will know that they have heard from God. Our utter dependence upon His grace will show.

Let us pray that God will make preaching the agent of transformation God intended it to be.

Get yourself up on a high mountain,
O Zion, bearer of good news,
Lift up your voice mightily,
O Jerusalem, bearer of good news;
Lift it up, do not fear.
Say to the cities of Judah,
"Here is your God!"
(Isa. 40:9 NASB)

When we preach, God just might do a miracle!

## • 6 •

## Christian Loafers

*Can We Get Them in Step?*

Faithfulness—you've preached on it; so have I. But have our sermons done much good? At a recent pastors' conference, several men shared their frustration about the casual attitude some believers have in serving the church. Every congregation can boast of a few dependable, joyful volunteers. Unfortunately, they are sometimes the exception rather than the rule.

The casually committed are those who habitually arrive late to every meeting. Some of them must even plan to be late. I'm sure they haven't heard the invocation of a morning service for years.

Then there are those who never let anyone know when they will be absent. Sunday school teachers, ushers, and committee workers simply don't show up for their assigned responsibilities. Consequently, someone has to scurry around looking for a harried replacement.

We're all acquainted with those who accept responsibilities but don't follow through. Jane promises to offer Donna a ride; John will see if Bill needs further counsel; Peter vows to write an important letter; Frank assures us he will be at the next committee meeting. But nothing happens—not this week or the next five.

Our congregations are also populated by those who justify their negligence with flimsy excuses. "We had company," someone will say. "The weather turned cold [or hot or windy or humid, depending on your location]," others say.

Such performances would not be tolerated in the secular world. Many believers who would never be late on Monday morning shirk

38

their Sunday duties without a twinge of conscience. Of course, we can't threaten to fire them.

## An Army of Volunteers

"Remember, these are all volunteers," someone once said to me. "You can't fire people who don't get paid. When you've got a volunteer army, you take what you can get."

So we continue with latecomers, promise breakers, and procrastinators. And our volunteer army limps along. Many of us can appreciate this parody of the hymn "Onward Christian Soldiers":

> Like a mighty turtle,
> Moves the church of God;
> Brothers, we are treading
> Where we've always trod.

In a recent *Atlantic Monthly* article, James Fallows bemoans the deterioration of the U.S. Army since the draft was abandoned. He quotes an essay published in 1980 by William Hauser, a retired colonel.

Hauser claims there are four elements sustaining the "will to fight." To learn *submission*, a soldier must repeat disagreeable tasks. To counter *fear*, he must know and trust his comrades. That will encourage him to fight alongside them instead of running in the wrong direction. To evoke *loyalty*, the Army requires that the men sleep, work, and eat together. They will eventually gain a sense of responsibility for one another's welfare. Finally, the army attempts to develop a sense of *pride* that will remind a man that others depend on him and value his contribution to the unit's safety and success. Thus he fights, hoping that he will not be brought home in a body bag.

Each of those qualities, however, has diminished with the volunteer force. Recruitment is now based largely on self-interest rather than on service to our nation. As a result, those who enlist are only casually committed. They are more interested in retirement benefits than in whether they are really prepared to fight.

Sound familiar? I think it's time we challenged the notion that the church is a volunteer army. Since when did God give us the option of enlisting? Does He discuss terms of commitment with us? Should faithfulness be expected only of those who get paid for their work?

Do we have the right to expect less on Sunday morning than we do on Monday morning?

## An Army Under Orders

Let's remind ourselves of some facts. First, we didn't choose Christ; He chose us. Jesus said, "You did not choose Me, but I chose you, and appointed you, that you should go and bear fruit" (John 15:16 NASB). As Commander in Chief, He has a role for each of us to play. We are, as Peter Marshall pointed out, "sealed under orders."

Our Commander decides how and where the battles should be fought. Paul learned submission and obedience by becoming Christ's bondslave. We can't ignore the divine call without becoming an outright deserter.

Second, faithfulness in small details promotes greater responsibility. "He who is faithful in a very little thing is faithful also in much; and he who is unrighteous in a very little thing is unrighteous also in much" (Luke 16:10 NASB).

As pastors, we wouldn't think of being late for a morning worship service. After all, it's a public event. But is it any less important to be on time for Sunday school or a counseling appointment? In the eyes of men, yes; in the eyes of God, no.

When it comes to seeking obedience from their children, parents care little whether they are working on minor or major tasks. It's the child's attitude of obedience that counts. Our heavenly Father shares the same sentiments. When we are unfaithful in "small" matters, we insult our Commander in Chief. He doesn't overlook apparently insignificant details. Even a cup of cold water offered in Christ's name merits reward.

Third, our motivation must be to please the Lord, not men. Paul wrote to Timothy, "No soldier in active service entangles himself in the affairs of everyday life, so that he may please the one who enlisted him as a soldier" (2 Tim. 2:4 NASB).

In Napoleon's army, men endured physical pain, illness, or even the sacrifice of an arm or leg just for an approving nod from their leader. Nothing will purify our motives like deciding to be obedient to Jesus, regardless of whether we are recognized in this world.

When washing the disciples' feet or preaching the Sermon on the Mount, Christ had the same motivation. He said, "I always do the things that are pleasing to [My Father]" (John 8:29 NASB). He wasn't playing the game of life for the benefit of His contemporaries. He did not consider Himself merely a volunteer but a humble servant compelled to do the Father's will.

Even the ungodly are faithful when they're getting paid. Christians, however, should be distinguished by their positive attitudes toward minor, unrewarded tasks. They should have the faith to believe that they will be rewarded in another world. After all, is it not our view of eternity that separates us from the values of this temporal world?

How can we, like Gideon, distinguish between the committed worker and the one who is along for the ride? We might want to grant an honorable discharge to anyone within the church who is shirking his or her responsibilities. It is better, though, for people to recognize their own deficiencies and dismiss themselves from active service.

Begin by establishing written performance standards for church positions. Those could include attendance, follow-through in responsibilities, and an outline of acceptable performance. Then share the guidelines with committees and board members. Let it be known that church leaders expect faithfulness. Let it also be known that the same leaders set an example of faithfulness to others.

Don't be afraid to let someone go. If you need to, leave a position vacant. That is a better option than filling it with another nonperformer. Look and wait for a qualified, reliable replacement. And pray. Then pray again.

Pastors, we need to display faithfulness in our own responsibilities. God will eventually provide a core of dedicated soldiers, willing to endure hardship for the cause of Christ. Increasing the number of dependable, qualified, and deeply committed believers starts with us.

A volunteer army will never do. Only one conscripted by a higher calling will have the determination to finish the task.

## • 7 •

# Church Splits

*When Are They Worth the Cost?*

I'm weary of hearing about church splits over trivial issues. In one church, a few men wanted their pastor to enforce a dress code and to conduct the services according to their liking. He didn't fully accommodate them. Because they thought their authority was slighted, small matters were magnified. Soon, everything the pastor did was wrong. His detractors scrutinized his sermons to find hidden meanings directed toward them.

The pastor resigned. He probably had the support of 90 percent of the congregation, but he grew tired of the hassle. He was not a fighter. He left an effective ministry because of a few disgruntled members. Just recently another pastor friend of mine did the same thing. Some of the leadership wanted his church to be a clone of a larger church in the same area. He could not take the constant comparisons, which he deemed to be unfair.

How long has it been since you heard that a church was divided because of the Virgin Birth or salvation by faith in Christ alone? Most of the strife I hear about concerns budgets, music, or leadership philosophy. Often, the real issue is who's in charge.

These resignations caused me to reflect on this question: What should a church member do if he or she wants to voice a legitimate complaint? Most of the people are not on a church board, yet they have deep feelings about the ministry of the church. If we are wise, we will find ways by which we can forestall some of these disagreements.

## What Usually Happens?

Unfortunately, many church members take one of two courses of action when they have a complaint. The first course is to share criticism with others in order to drum up support. The tongue is the greatest cause for division within the church. "And the tongue is a fire, the very world of iniquity; the tongue is set among our members as that which defiles the entire body, and sets on fire the course of our life, and is set on fire by hell" (James 3:6 NASB).

To use our tongues to rally support for our viewpoints is to spread the fires of hell within the church. Sometimes the church is already polarized over an issue before the elders or the pastor even know about the problem. Certainly, there is a time to speak, but that time does not come as frequently as some people think it does.

An equally disastrous procedure is to bring up the matter in a church business meeting. Often, this is done to score points publicly even when no attempt has been made to resolve the issue privately. Any matter that can be dealt with between one or two members or that could be cared for through other legitimate channels should never be mentioned for public discussion.

I know a pastor who was humiliated in a church business meeting; he had to endure totally unexpected personal criticisms. Surely Satan must rejoice in church meetings where everyone feels he has the freedom to air his favorite gripe.

We must instruct our congregations on the need for unity, but at the same time we should allow for dialogue regarding disagreements. If not, resentment and misunderstanding will only build. People must feel that their complaints have been heard.

## What Can Be Done?

First, *we ourselves must set an example of submission.* Paul wrote, "Be subject to one another in the fear of Christ" (Eph. 5:21 NASB). I wince when I hear a pastor teach his congregation to submit to authority when he believes he is an exception to the rule. "I'm accountable to God alone" sounds pious, but it can be poisonous.

The New Testament teaches that a congregation is to have a plurality of godly leaders with no one person assuming the role of dictator. Though some congregations are polite enough to tolerate authoritarianism, others chafe under the strain. Individuals know that their input is worthless because the pastor receives his instruction privately from God.

Or at times a pastor might be defensive, unwilling to accept criticism. He might listen politely, but in his heart he is convinced that whatever is said is untrue. We all find it difficult to see ourselves objectively; some pastors find it impossible. Every comment is deflected, unable to penetrate the mind or the heart.

Don't be surprised, then, when believers feel frustrated in their attempts to get their points across. If the pastor is a law unto himself, why cannot they be? Like pastor, like people.

No doubt many churches have split because God wanted to bring the pastor and the congregation to a place of mutual submission. But when the pastor isn't responsive to the authority of his board, the congregation often rejects the authority of the pastor as well. Meanwhile, the gap between the pastor and the board widens.

As church leaders, we must set an example of humility. We cannot exercise authority unless we ourselves are under authority. That does not mean that we back down over every issue; certainly, there are times when we must defend ourselves. But how, when, and why are important.

Second, *we must teach that Matthew 18:15–16 applies to all kinds of disagreements.* "And if your brother sins, go and reprove him in private; if he listens to you, you have won your brother. But if he does not listen to you, take one or two more with you, so that by the mouth of two or three witnesses every fact may be confirmed."

The believer is responsible to go directly to the person against whom he has a grievance. If the issue involves specific sin, then there is an obligation to go to the person even if he is a church leader. But Paul warned, "Do not receive an accusation against an elder except on the basis of two or three witnesses" (1 Tim. 5:19 NASB).

If the issue remains unresolved, then others—particularly other members of the church board—must become involved. And the elder or pastor must defer to their authority.

But what about opposition to a building program, the pastor's salary, or the length of his sermons? To discuss such disagreements with members of the congregation sows seeds of discord that grieve the heart of God. Here also, members should go directly to the person responsible, even if it means a trip to the pastor's office or writing him a signed letter.

At this point, our attitude as pastors is critical. If we ignore what is said or if we dismiss the criticism without learning from it, we may be encouraging the concerned member to try another approach—to recruit other members to his position through gossip.

I've found that an honest discussion clears the air and can cement a relationship, even if the disagreement persists. There's something gratifying about having someone else try earnestly to see your point of view, even if he remains unconvinced. What is difficult is when a parishioner thinks he has not even been heard.

That doesn't mean we have to agree with everything that is said to us. But I've often found that there may be more truth to criticism than we are willing to admit. It's easy to listen politely but then dismiss what has been said without thoughtful consideration and prayer.

In my opinion, if a church member takes a matter of concern to a member of the board, that is as far as he or she should go in their criticisms of the pastor. Even if the board fails in their responsibility, members do not have a biblical mandate to begin petitions, write letters, and use the telephone to drum up support for their cause. The New Testament pattern is that a church be led by a plurality of godly leaders. If you cannot agree with the action of the board, you might want to think about worshiping elsewhere.

Of course, I don't mean to stifle profitable discussion among church members about improving the ministry or talking about matters in preparation for a church business meeting. We should expect our people to discuss various ministries within the church. But once a decision is made, there must be submission to the will of those in authority.

## Waiting for God

In a day when people demand their rights, it's difficult for a congregation to submit to church leaders and wait for God to work His will even in controversial decisions. Sometimes a member of the congregation might have an idea that is correct, but the timing is wrong. We forget that God works among His people despite diversity of opinion and imperfections of church leaders.

That fact applies to those of us who are on a church board as well. I've had to submit to the will of leaders even on those occasions when I may have had a difference of opinion. God is honored when we are willing to set aside disagreements over non-biblical issues for the unity and harmony of the body.

Only heaven will reveal the damage done to the body of Christ by members of the congregation who feel called to correct all the faults of the church or to campaign for their pet grievances. We have too many people who believe that their spiritual gift is that of criticism.

I fear for those who are determined to force the resignation of a man of God by petty criticisms. I fear for those who have divided a congregation because of intransigence over a building program or the proposed budget.

Yes, there are times when a church split is justified, perhaps even necessary. But let's be sure that it's over a clear biblical issue and not just a preference we hold dear.

Paul wrote, "If any man destroys the temple of God, God will destroy him, for the temple of God is holy, and that is what you are" (1 Cor. 3:17 NASB). The word *temple* refers to the congregation of believers. God says He will destroy the one who destroys the work of the church. Often, He grants that person a hard and bitter heart, or He may use other means of discipline.

Dr. Paul Brand says that white blood cells, the armed forces of the body, guard against invaders. When the body's been cut, these cells abruptly stop their aimless wandering and home in from all different directions on the scene of the battle. As if they have a sense of smell, they hurry through tissue via the most direct route. When they arrive, many of them give their lives to kill the bacteria. They subject themselves to the good of the larger organism that determines their duties. If a cell should lose its loyalty and cling to its own life, it shares the benefits of the body but sets up a rival organism called cancer.

Our churches are filled with parasites who benefit from the ministry but who refuse to submit themselves to the leader of the organism. As a result, the body is cancerous, weak, and unprepared for battle. Sometimes, so much energy is spent in resolving internal conflict that there is no time to confront the world with Jesus Christ.

If we're guilty of dividing the body, we'd better repent. When we disagree with church leaders, we should talk to God rather than to our friends. He is able to direct His own church in His own time and in His own way. To destroy the temple of God is to toy with the wrath of God.

# · 8 ·

# Politics

---

## *Where Should We Draw the Line?*

Some preachers have jumped into the political arena with both feet, causing us to rethink our stand on political involvement. Christians by the hundreds of thousands are becoming politically active. The religious right is a force that cannot be ignored.

There are good arguments in favor of political activism. Americans are entitled to work through the political process to effect change. Why should evangelicals sell out to radical feminists, gay liberationists, and abortionists? We have an agenda of our own and a right to be heard. Perhaps the ballot box does speak louder than words.

What better way to get our message across than to organize and vote the humanists out of office? Why not elect those who would enact laws that reflect a more biblical approach to morality? In a democracy, political power talks.

Then there is the precedent set by liberal religious organizations such as the World Council of Churches, which uses political clout to accomplish social and economic change. Why can't we do the same?

Evangelicals, often marginalized as an embarrassing anachronism in American history, have finally tasted political power. With the rise of the religious right, liberal politicians have had to take stock of their positions. After all, some people think that Christians, if well organized, can "throw the bums out."

I agree that we can be grateful for every Christian in politics; we ought to support organizations that attempt to educate the religious constituency about the issues being debated in Washington. Christians ought to make their influence felt in local and national elections and to speak up for what they believe. Often, we've lost crucial battles by default.

Yet, I am troubled because I believe that we are being tempted to fight the battle in a way that undermines the very message we want the world to hear. Ask the average person what Christians believe, and he will give you a long agenda: they are opposed to abortion, hate gays, and want television programs censored. He will also probably say that they want to impose their agenda on everyone.

Regardless of whether such a characterization is fair, we are stuck with it. And perhaps the reason is because we have fought too many battles under the Christian banner; we have needlessly confused the issues and have often done so with bigotry, anger, and a victim mentality. We have often not represented Christ with clarity and charity.

I am troubled when I see ministers speak out on matters that would be better left to politicians. As a minister, I have no right to endorse a political candidate, even if he happens to be a Christian who holds a biblical worldview. Speaking as a private citizen is one thing, but to use the pulpit as a platform for political endorsement is another. We must remember that we have a responsibility to speak to all political parties; we must stand for truth in all walks of life, and we dare not confuse the Cross with partisan politics.

But there are other dangers as well.

## The Dangers of Political Involvement

As was already indicated, biblical and political issues tend to be mixed together as one lump. If we label all of these issues "Christian," we can easily be misunderstood. Indeed, the message of the Cross can be severely compromised when it is encumbered by a host of agendas.

Abortion is a biblical issue, we can all unite in opposition to the arbitrary killing of human life. But what about tax breaks for families and term limits for congressmen? These and a half-dozen other issues have been supported under the Christian banner. They are worthy issues, perhaps, but such legislation can be supported by many non-Christians, too. The problem is that people no longer think of Christ when they think of Christianity; it is a political agenda that comes to mind.

Second, I fear that political reformation could subtly substitute for spiritual transformation. Of course, we all favor laws that reflect biblical morality. But even such progress falls far short of the real answer to our national decay. Ultimately, it is only the gospel of Christ that can stem the tide of moral decadence.

Suppose that prayer is restored in the public schools. In our society, such prayer would be based on the lowest common denominator of all religions. Christ's name would not be mentioned, hardly a credit to the One whose sacrifice is the only means of reconciling our nation to God. We would be forcing unbelieving teachers and students to recite a prayer with their mouths, though they resent it in their hearts. Most countries in Europe still have prayer in schools, but that has not kept the church strong, nor has it prevented moral and spiritual stagnation. Might we do better to restore prayer back to our churches instead?

Suppose that teaching creationism in our public schools was mandatory. That would hardly make our public schools Christian. Whatever lip service such laws would achieve, it would fall short of the change of heart God desires.

Civil religion can help bring about a moral reformation. But at the same time, it gives a false sense of security. We may honor God with our lips, but our hearts are far from Him. We know that the law cannot save an individual; neither can it save a country. As ministers, we must teach our people never to settle for less than the radical transformation that the gospel can bring.

Third, what if we simply don't have the political power to bring about reform? And when we openly join with those who explicitly deny the gospel in our effort to turn America back to God, are we not thereby leaning on a broken reed? The issues that unite us with other religions cannot possibly be the primary mission of the church.

Yes, we might win some battles and make a few reforms. But our gains are dependent on the ballot box. In a democratic political process, one reaction will always spawn another. Someone once said that "the art of politics is the art of destroying your enemies." To fight moral issues with political muscle is a high-risk venture that fluctuates each passing year. Fighting spiritual battles with carnal weapons is even more sure to fail.

Christ was largely silent about political matters. He never encouraged a revolution against Rome. Paul did not speak out against slavery lest Christianity be charged with causing political upheaval. Instead, he taught slaves to "regard their own masters as worthy of all honor so that the name of God and our doctrine may not be spoken against" (1 Tim. 6:1 NASB). Admittedly, in those days slavery was so interwoven with the fabric of society that overthrowing the practice would have been impossible. Indeed, in later centuries Christianity was the force that battled slavery. But the point is that Paul did not want to identify with external political and social changes that might detract from the purity of the gospel.

Of course, I agree that our day is different. We are encouraged to be involved in the political process. But we must choose our battles carefully lest the Cross of Christ be linked with many political causes. We must gain consensus with all those inclined to agree with us for political ends, but the message of the gospel must often be shielded from such associations.

## Our Response

What should be our response in the face of the moral and spiritual decline of our nation?

First, we must admit that the true church is defenseless in the world. We are strangers and pilgrims who cannot afford to pin our hopes on the fortunes of the erratic political process. God alone is our defender.

Fortunately, our strength does not depend on a political majority. The fortunes of a nation often depend on a godly minority, as in the case of Gideon. If God does not take up our cause and fight in our behalf, we shall eventually be destroyed. We must seek His face, humbly asking that He would, even at this late hour, grant us mercy.

Second, we must understand the exalted role the church plays in the political affairs of this world. The bride of Christ holds back the coming judgment of God. The world, if I might humbly suggest, has no idea how much it owes the church. As for God, the church is number one on His agenda. Everything He does in this world is somehow related to the body of Christ; thus, everything shall someday be summed up in Him (Eph. 1:10).

Therefore, our spiritual condition as a church determines in a large measure God's blessing or judgment on our nation. Too often we have blamed the humanists for the moral decay around us without realizing that God may be judging us through them. It was God's prophet Jonah, not the pagan sailors, who caused the storm on the Mediterranean.

If we are able to turn our nation back to God, it most likely should be attributed to a godly remnant's intercessory prayer for spiritual revival. The righteousness that exalts a nation is the fruit of repentance. God certainly does not owe us a revival, but if we cry out to Him, He might yet show us mercy.

Of course, prayer must be combined with action. Parents must become involved in their school systems, we must stand against the infiltration of pornography into our homes and schools, and we must most assuredly fight against abortion. But we must fight like Christ, because at the end of the day, people must see Jesus. Our attitude is as important as the issue we are addressing.

So, as ministers we must address the moral issues of our time with courage and clarity. Our positions on abortion and homosexual perspectives must be knowledgeably analyzed and critiqued. Whenever the laws of the state conflict with clear biblical convictions, we must obey God rather than men, even if it means going to jail.

We must not be intimidated by those who wish to silence the mouths of ministers under the guise of separation of church and state. But we must also remember that our message is not a political agenda but the full biblical mandate of submission to the will of God.

But—and this is important—we must not be angry and bigoted in our criticisms. Moreover, we must remember that our primary responsibility is to share the good news of God's love and forgiveness. We must be agents of healing and not division, of understanding and not distortion. In short, we must represent Christ, living His values and message. We must keep the Cross at the forefront of our minds, our hearts, and our ministries.

To fulfill such a calling, we cannot be wedded publicly to any political party. Of course, we vote, but as ministers we don't tell our congregation how they should vote. In our fallen world, even born-again candidates can disappoint us. Each party has its own peculiar blend of good and evil. We must condemn evil wherever it is found, without any indebtedness to a party or a candidate.

The revivals of John Wesley and George Whitefield resulted in great social changes. God brought them about by the miracle of the new birth. He prefers to work from the inside out. What political power could never do, the conviction and the power of the Holy Spirit accomplished.

I believe it's time for us as individuals and churches to seek the Lord with repentant hearts. If we look to Washington, we will be disappointed. We can only submit ourselves unreservedly to the will of God and become personal and corporate witnesses to His power in our decadent society.

If our problems were political, a political solution would be all that was needed. But if they are spiritual, they must be addressed from that vantage point. If we, as God's people, repent, He may yet restore the years that the locusts have eaten. For in God we have the greatest power that could ever be unleashed. Politics is the art of achieving the possible, but faith is the art of achieving the impossible.

This nation needs to experience the impossible.

# • 9 •

# Envy

---

## *How Should We Live in the Shadow of Success?*

A fable tells how Satan's emissaries were trying to tempt a holy man who lived in the Libyan desert. Try as they might, the demons could not get the man to sin. The seductions of the flesh and the onslaught of doubts and fears left him unmoved.

Angered by their failure, Satan stepped forward. "Your methods are too crude," he said. "Just watch." He whispered in the holy man's ear, "Your brother has just been made Bishop of Alexandria."

Instantly, a malignant scowl clouded the holy man's face.

"Envy," Satan said to his cohorts, "is our final weapon for those who seek holiness."

### Making Comparisons

As pastors, we struggle with the same enticements as the people in our congregations. But because our ministries are public, our most powerful temptation may be envy. We all know how much it hurts to be compared with a pastor who is more successful.

"You're OK, but you're no Swindoll," a parishioner tells us with a touch of finality. Or a board member asks, "Why aren't we growing like Willow Creek's congregation?"

But such comments are passing, and we can handle them with a bit of good humor. It's more difficult when your congregation prefers your assistant pastor's preaching—or when the church next door is bursting at the seams while yours is slowly declining. Then it's easy to become critical and defensive. We say we have "a ministry of depth, not a numbers racket." Or we accuse the congregation of liking the assistant's preaching better because he "tickles their ears."

Our fallen nature loathes to be cast in bad light. It's difficult to rejoice with those who are more successful. At times, we even have quiet satisfaction when we learn about others' failures; by comparison we think we are doing better.

What aggravates the problem is that God's blessings seem so inconsistent. We see a church with phenomenal growth even though its pastor is a dull preacher who does little to inspire his congregation. At the same time, another church with an excellent preacher and good public relations skills may decline in membership.

Some pastors' theology is weak, their methods of fundraising are suspect, and their personal lives are in shambles, yet they are blessed with growth and money. Meanwhile, other pastors with integrity and faithfulness can't raise enough money to paint the church. No wonder a missionary once said to me, "Have you ever noticed how often God puts His hand on the wrong person?"

It's hard not to wonder why; it's hard not to envy.

### The Strength of the Poison

Envy will cripple any pastor and his ministry. First, it erodes faith. Jesus asked the Pharisees, who were men pleasers, "How can you believe, when you receive glory from one another, and you do not seek the glory that is from the one and only God?" (John 5:44 NASB). With their eyes on one another, they were unable to focus their eyes on God. The envious are in no position to please God. They are not free to believe wholeheartedly in Christ.

Second, envy produces isolationism. A pastor who fears the success of others will withdraw from fellowship and cooperation with other churches. He may say his reason for separation is the need for doctrinal purity. At times, important doctrinal matters are at stake and separatism is necessary. But if our hidden motives were exposed, much of our separation is rooted in the fear of allowing our congregations to be blessed outside the walls of our own little kingdom.

Although the Pharisees said they were crucifying Christ for doctrinal reasons, that was not the *real* reason they condemned Christ. Pilate discerned their underlying motive: "For he knew that because of envy they had delivered Him up" (Matt. 27:18 NASB). Envy was the motive; theology was the smoke screen.

Paul had a similar experience in Pisidian Antioch, where his preaching drew large crowds. "But when the Jews saw the crowds, they were filled with jealousy, and began contradicting the things spoken by Paul, and were blaspheming" (Acts 13:45 NASB). Once again, theology was the excuse for antagonism, but the motivation was less noble.

Writing to the Philippians, Paul discerned that some people were preaching Christ out of envy and strife, hoping to make him look bad. Yet, he rejoiced that Christ was preached, even though their motives were sinful (Phil. 1:12–18).

An envious person may fear unfavorable comparison so much that he works behind the scenes to sabotage a colleague's ministry. If he operates carefully, his hidden motive may never come to light. This, of course, makes the judgment seat of Christ all the more important, for God shall expose the motives of men's hearts.

King Saul was not as careful to hide his jealousy. He was so angered by the comparison in the cheers of the crowd, "Saul has slain his thousands, And David his ten thousands" (1 Sam. 18:7), that he became obsessed with killing his young rival. God's response was to send a demon to trouble him, evidently so he would be goaded into repentance. Instead, Saul eventually committed suicide.

Once envy has found a home in the human heart, it resists eviction. Even death may seem more attractive than conceding success to someone who is younger and less qualified. Don't ever underestimate the depths to which we are able to sink in order to make ourselves look good.

## Neutralizing the Poison

How do we overcome this deceitful monster? We must treat envy for the sin it is. It is rebellion against God's providential leading in the lives of His children. An envious person is saying God has no right to bless someone else more than himself.

Jesus told a parable about a landowner who agreed to pay a denarius a day to workers who arrived early. Others who came later in the day didn't haggle about their wages but were willing to trust the landowner's fairness.

At the end of the day, those who came last were the first to be paid. Each received a denarius. Those who had worked since morning assumed they'd be paid more, but they were shocked when they, too, received one denarius (Matt. 20:1–12).

Unfair.

Imagine an employer paying those who arrive at 3:00 P.M. the same as those who show up on time. But Jesus gave the story a surprising twist: it was fair because the first workers got what they'd agreed on. If the landowner wanted to pay the latecomers that much, too, he was at liberty to do so.

Speaking for the landowner, who represents God, Jesus said, "Is it not lawful for me to do what I wish with what is my own? Or is your eye envious because I am generous?" (v. 15). God can do what He wishes with His own. He can be more generous with others, and we have no right to complain. Envy is rebellion against His sovereign rights.

Envy is also a sin against God's goodness. Whatever we have, be it little or much, it is a gift of God. When Jesus Christ eclipsed John the Baptist's ministry and, therefore, his cousin in the flesh was tempted to envy, he rightly replied, "A man can receive nothing, unless it has been given him from heaven" (John 3:27 NASB). Envy is based on the assumption that our abilities and gifts are something we're entitled to have.

Envy is a sin that lashes out against God's goodness and sovereignty. It's the pot telling the potter how to make other vessels. Francis Schaeffer said there is no such thing as small people and big people, only consecrated people and unconsecrated people. One pastor said, "When I finally accepted the fact that God did not want me to be well known, I began to experience His blessing."

Paul taught that it was God who determined where we would fit within the body of Christ. "But one and the same Spirit works all these things, distributing to each one individually *just as He wills*" (1 Cor. 12:11 NASB, emphasis added). To be dissatisfied with our gift is to be dissatisfied with our God.

Comparisons of ministries or preachers are almost always sinful. We must not be like the disciples who asked, "Who will be the greatest in the kingdom of heaven?" The fact is, we don't know. We can

easily see that a skyscraper is taller than a small apartment building, but if we compare both buildings against the height of a distant
star, there's not much difference between them. Likewise, the differences among us fade into oblivion when we compare ourselves with
Christ.

God wants to give us humble satisfaction with our place in His
vineyard. Having any place in the vineyard affirms His mercy and
grace. To envy those who are given greater blessing is to imbibe a
spirit of thanklessness and rebellion.

Moses was a Spirit-filled man, but God multiplied his ministry in
the lives of seventy elders who were given the gift of prophecy. Two of
those elders, Eldad and Medad, were particularly gifted and proph-
esied in the camp. When a young man came running to Moses and
told him the news, Joshua said, "Moses, my lord, restrain them."

But Moses said to him, "Are you jealous for my sake? Would that
all the Lord's people were prophets, that the Lord would put His
Spirit upon them!" (Num. 11:28–29 NASB).

You can't destroy a man who rejoices in the success of others. He
has a proper perspective of himself and his God. He can rejoice in
those who are more successful. He's thankful for even the small op-
portunities to serve because he hasn't lost the wonder of the Father's
care. And a genuine smile breaks forth when you tell him that his
brother has been appointed Bishop of Alexandria.

# · 10 ·

# Burnout

*Can Wet Wood Still Be Ignited?*

A church janitor was heard to say, "The blower still works, but the fire has gone out." He was discussing a problem with the furnace, but the parishioner who overheard him thought he was speaking about the pastor.

One definition of burnout is "a syndrome of emotional exhaustion, depersonalization, and reduced personal accomplishment that can occur among individuals who do 'people work' of some kind." Its symptoms include increased fatigue, tiredness even after a good night's sleep, loss of interest in one's work, and a pessimistic, critical spirit often accompanied by withdrawal, depression, and a feeling of futility.

According to Archibald D. Hart, dean of the graduate school of psychology at Fuller Theological Seminary, however, burnout may be beneficial as a warning that something has gone wrong. It may intervene and take you out of a harmful environment when you're on the road to stressful destruction.

"It instantly slows you down and produces a state of lethargy and disengagement," Hart says. "The system 'gives out' before it 'blows up.'"

Whereas stress is characterized by overinvolvement, burnout is characterized by withdrawal and a loss of meaning and hope. Regardless of what the person does, the rewards seem too small to bother. It can lead to depression.

## Causes of Burnout

One study indicated that one-third of the pastors surveyed had considered leaving the ministry because of burnout. Although burnout can occur in all professions, ministers are particularly vulnerable. One reason may be the conflict of roles.

We are expected to be good preachers, counselors, and organizers; know something about publicity; and have the fine art of loving people and showing it in our relationships. When these responsibilities are not accompanied by rewards, the pushes and pulls of those expectations can lead to a sense of futility and despair. Because people come to the pastor to *get* rather than to *give*, his emotional resources can easily become depleted.

Second, the pastor is often alone in his struggles. Though the members of the church can speak freely to him about their problems, he is not free to reciprocate. As J. Grant Swank Jr. says, "Pastors wonder who is going to pull the supports out from under them if they open up, if they are honest about the tensions of the pastorate. Consequently, in too many cases it is very hard for the minister to discover a partner in ministry other than the spouse."[1]

If the pastor's marriage is falling apart or if his children are an embarrassment, he feels trapped and unable to extricate himself from his emotional lows. Soon, he wonders how he can be of help to others when he himself has such a strong sense of failure.

All of us have feelings of inadequacy. And we are not helped when we are compared with the television preachers who are able to draw large crowds and money. Though our faults are well known to our congregations, the people hear of only the successes of radio and television preachers.

If we preach one poor sermon, everyone knows it; if we get indignant at a board meeting, word gets around. Soon, we think we are unappreciated. If we are particularly sensitive to criticism, we will try to overachieve to please everyone. If we don't receive adequate emotional and spiritual compensation for our efforts, we will be left wondering if it's all worthwhile.

Dr. David Congo, associated with H. Norman Wright's Family Counseling Clinic in Santa Ana, California, says the ministry can be represented by either a "rat race" or a "relay race." Both require a great deal of energy, but a rat race has no clear sense of purpose. A relay race, however, has direction, a prescribed course, cooperation, and team spirit. The pastor in a rat race often feels like a victim controlled by his situation. It's hard to say whether that is the cause of burnout or its result, but there's a direct relationship in either case.

Congo lists four personality types linked to burnout:

- those with a high need for approval
- the workaholic
- the unassertive, passive victim
- those with a "messiah complex"[2]

All of us are tempted to give beyond our own spiritual and emotional resources to be thought of as successful. The result may be our feeling fulfilled. Or it may do the opposite—lead to inner anger and disillusionment.

If a pastor feels unappreciated, his response may be to "cop out." He absorbs many hurts, each of which diminishes his self-esteem, which, in turn, contributes to an attitude of "Why should I care about you, because you don't care about me?" At that point, either the fire goes out or it is stoked with anger and becomes the fire that destroys rather than the fire that cleanses.

The simple fact is that many pastors have unresolved anger that they are unwilling to admit. This anger is often cloaked with phrases such as "righteous indignation" or "ministerial earnestness," but it is there nevertheless. Often, they are angry because as children they felt disconnected from their parents, or perhaps they are now resentful because the ministry has been hard and thankless. As was already mentioned, the rewards for their efforts are simply not worth the cost.

## Cures for Burnout

What is the cure? The usual advice follows these lines: exercise regularly, get proper rest, take a vacation, and reorganize your priorities. Those suggestions would undoubtedly contribute to recovery, but often the root goes deeper.

Who of us hasn't taken time to relax, only to discover we can't because of a nagging sense of guilt or failure? What about the anxiety we feel as we anticipate the next board meeting, when our new proposal will be discussed? And how can we enjoy our vacation if we suspect a member of the board might undermine our leadership while we're away?

There is a surer path.

The first part of the answer to burnout is to be controlled from within rather than from without. We must be satisfied with doing the will of God rather than being overly dependent on the opinions of men. That may require getting away from it all for a week's retreat or even taking a leave of absence to get it all together. But it is in that quiet, inner world that we meet God and that the answer will eventually be found. Remember, burnout is something we do to ourselves and only secondarily something that the ministry does to us.

In *Ordering Your Private World*, Gordon MacDonald describes the difference between a person who is driven (such as King Saul) and a person who is called (such as John the Baptist). A driven person is gratified only by accomplishments and its symbols. He often possesses a volcanic anger that erupts anytime he senses opposition or disloyalty. When he cannot achieve his goals in public ministry, he becomes disillusioned because his private life is left empty and wanting.

John realized that the crowds did not belong to him; he ministered as the Lord saw fit. He didn't need the exhilaration that comes through public affirmation, nor did he see himself out of focus. He might have been tempted to think of himself as a great preacher, but he directed the crowds to Christ: "He must increase, but I must decrease" (v. 30).

John's contentment was not built on his career; he could find stability in his private, inner world. Pastors who neglect their inner world soon find themselves unable to cope with the weight of the external demands placed upon them.

Burnout may be a reminder to develop our inner world. Spending time in quietness before the Lord and asking His guidance in those areas of neglect and failure could be just the experience we need. Perhaps those of us who say yes to too many invitations will discover we weren't called to save the world. We don't have to live up to the expectations of our congregations; we can be content serving in faithfulness within the limitations of our gifts and aptitudes.

In 1749, Jonathan Edwards chose to break with the tradition of the day and insist that only those who gave evidence of conversion should be allowed to participate in Communion. Though he wrote a book to defend his views, few read it. Instead, disgruntled members took up the cause and garnered enough support to oppose Edwards. The members of his church openly reproached him, accusing him of being more concerned about himself than the good of the church. They held meetings in his absence, and discord was sown far and wide.

Finally, on June 19, 1750, a council, consisting of many churches, met and recommended that the relationship between Edwards and his church be dissolved. When the church itself voted, many of Edwards' supporters stayed away. In the final tally, 230 members voted for his dismissal; about 29 people voted for him to stay. The deed was done.

How did Edwards accept this harsh and unfair decision? A close friend who observed him, wrote:

> That faithful witness received the shock, unshaken. I never saw the least symptoms of displeasure in his countenance the whole week but *he appeared like a man of God, whose happiness was out of the reach of his enemies* and whose treasure was not only a future but a present good, overbalancing all imaginable ills of life, even to the astonishment of many who could not be at rest without his dismission.[3] (emphasis added)

Of course it hurt. Indeed, Edwards felt betrayed by his friends and lonely in being "separated from the people between whom and me there once was the greatest union." Yet he also saw in this the providence of God. God would use him to do missionary work among the Indians and to write books that would benefit future generations.

Years later, one of the dissenters confessed that the real reason behind opposition to Edwards was pride. "I now see that I was very much influenced by vast pride, self-sufficiency, ambition, and vanity." But it was too late.

My point is that Edwards could accept unfair treatment in the ministry because *his happiness in God was beyond the reach of his enemies.* Here was a man who learned what Martin Lloyd-Jones would say many years later: "Don't let your happiness depend on preaching, for the day will come when you can no longer preach. Find your happiness in God who will be with us to the end."

The second part of the answer to burnout is to confide in close friends. Every pastor should have several people, perhaps outside his congregation, with whom he can be honest about his struggles. We all need the acceptance and confidentiality of friends who will listen carefully and pray fervently.

During days when we're unsteady emotionally, everything is distorted. We desperately need the perspective of those who have maintained their emotional equilibrium. Blessed is the pastor who can be open with at least a few friends during his emotional blackouts.

James B. Scott experienced burnout and resigned from his church. He wrote, "The most difficult part of the death of a dream was the feeling of loss and fear of not knowing if anything would ever come along to replace the loss." But eventually he realized that the ministry was in God's hands, not his. He continued, "Brokenness and healing has, by the power of God, produced unexpected results in my life. Strange how the pain of brokenness can miraculously bring about fullness and a tenacity of power and resources unknown previously."[4]

Many of us need once again to experience the inner power of God. There, in His presence, we must find meaning and tranquillity within rather than being sustained by approval from without. God wants us to find our joy coming from Him rather than from the unpredictable, often conflicting attitudes of men.

Sometimes, we may not be able to pinpoint the cause of burnout. Even so, we must interpret it as a reminder from God that our inner life needs special attention. "In quietness and in confidence shall be your strength" (Isa. 30:15 KJV). C. S. Lewis says the Lord shouts to us in our pains, but, I might add, He also speaks to us in our emotional doldrums.

Jesus demonstrated an inner satisfaction that enabled Him to cope with the stresses of His ministry. When a huge crowd gathered to hear Him, He disappointed them by going to another town and leaving them waiting (Mark 1:37–38). When He learned that Lazarus was sick, He stayed away two extra days, knowing that the will of God was being accomplished despite the disappointment of His friends Martha and Mary (John 11:6).

Christ never seemed to be in a hurry because He cared only about pleasing the Father. We must learn from Him the importance of playing the game for the coach, not for the fickle applause of the fans.

Burnout may mean that fresh coals must be offered on the altar of the heart. The God of Elijah is able to ignite even wet wood if it is laid out before Him in submission and anticipation.

Burnout need never be permanent if we are willing to wait for God to rekindle the flame.

# • 11 •

# The Church and the World

## *Who Is Influencing Whom?*

Recent Gallup polls have uncovered conflicting trends in our society: religion is on the upswing, but so is crime and immorality. George Gallup calls it "a giant paradox that religion is showing clear signs of revival even as the country is ridden with rising crime and other problems regarded as antithetical to religious piety."

Addressing a national seminar of Southern Baptist leaders, Gallup said, "We find there is very little difference in ethical behavior between churchgoers and those who are not active religiously. The levels of lying, cheating, and stealing are remarkably similar in both groups."

Eight out of ten Americans consider themselves Christians, Gallup said, yet only about half of them could identify the person who gave the Sermon on the Mount, and fewer still could recall five of the Ten Commandments. Only two of ten said they would be willing to suffer for their faith. Many Christian university students have adopted a "silent contract," kindly refusing to share their faith to fit in with the politically correct policies of the university. Thus, the desire to graduate is more important to them than representing Christ and taking the rap for it. Unlike the early church, few Christians think it a badge of honor to suffer for the suffering Savior.

What an indictment of American Christianity to have religion up while morality is down. Let's not excuse ourselves just because we suspect that the majority of those interviewed were not born-again believers.

Within evangelicalism is a distressing drift toward accepting a Christianity that does not demand a life-changing walk with God. Thanks to our limited knowledge of church history, many evangelicals don't realize that the church has always been an island of righteousness in a sea of paganism. The early Christians did not have the benefit of a sympathetic culture or government; they expected persecution and got it. But, as a result, they "turned their world upside down." We are proving that it is difficult to rear saints who are willing to suffer when we have become accustomed to an affluent culture.

### Religion à la Carte

Like the nominally religious person, we choose what we will believe and how we will act without much concern for what the Bible teaches. F. H. Henry wrote, "Millions of Protestants, many evangelicals among them, choose and change their churches as they do their airline—for convenience of travel, comfort, and economy." For us, as well as for the world, it's religion à la carte.

What can account for this? Since evangelicalism became popular a few decades ago, many people have felt free to identify with it at no personal cost. The stigma of Christianity is gone, but so is its power.

Within the evangelical camp is a growing trend toward accommodation—selecting what we like from the Bible and leaving the rest. We've been so caught up in the spirit of our age that we change colors like a chameleon to blend in with the latest worldly hue.

When gay rights activists argue that homosexuality is but an "alternate sexual preference," we find evangelicals writing books agreeing that the Bible doesn't condemn homosexuality. They say the Old Testament passages are a part of the law that doesn't apply today and that Paul was condemning only those who turned to homosexuality, not those who grew up that way.

When the feminists press their demands for equality, some preachers "restudy" the New Testament and discover that Paul didn't really mean what he wrote. They conclude that the husband is not the head of the wife and that women have the right to be ordained. Even more frightening is one evangelical's conclusion that Paul's view of women was just plain wrong.

When a socialistic mood sweeps the country, we have Christians who advocate the application of a Marxist theory for the redistribution of wealth. And when the peace movement gained momentum, some evangelicals jumped on that bandwagon, too.

I agree that we must examine our understanding of the Bible in relation to modern issues. But if we accommodate Scripture to whatever wind is blowing, we will become so absorbed by our culture that we will have nothing to say to it. In our zeal to be relevant, we will have lost our prophetic voice.

I'm reminded of the boy who bought a canary and put it in the same cage as a sparrow, hoping the sparrow would learn to sing. After three days, he gave up in disgust. The sparrow didn't sound like the canary; instead, the canary sounded just like the sparrow.

In *The Great Evangelical Disaster*, Francis Schaeffer says, "Here is the great evangelical disaster—the failure of the evangelical world to stand for truth as truth. . . . The evangelical church has accommodated to the world spirit of the age."[1]

However much we fault German theologian Rudolf Bultmann for rejecting the parts of the Bible that did not suit his fancy, we do the same when it comes to practicing biblical truth. Our actions show that we believe that scriptural authority rests with us and not with the text.

What is the result of this accommodation that picks and chooses from a religious smorgasbord? Society is being overrun by the cults, inundated with pornography, and destroyed by abortion on demand.

There are almost as many divorces within the church as outside of it. Sexual perversions of every kind are found within the church community, too. As Gallup suggests, the ethical behavior of those who attend church and those who do not is remarkably similar.

The new philosophy that "God wants you to be rich, happy, and healthy" has appealed to a generation that is quick to accept the benefits of Christianity without its painful obedience. Like a child standing by a slot machine hoping he can win the jackpot with a single coin, many churchgoers expect maximum return from minimum commitment. When they are not healed or don't get a promotion, they take their quarter and go elsewhere.

## Our Response

How should we respond to such an attitude? Perhaps we have to begin by returning to the gospel as found in the New Testament. Many of us are weary of "decisional regeneration" whereby we pronounce people saved because they have walked an aisle or filled out a decision card. We forget the words of Christ, "Every plant which My heavenly Father did not plant shall be rooted up" (Matt. 15:13 NASB).

I'm not saying that we should add stipulations to the free offer of the gospel, but that we must not think that people are regenerated because they tell us they are or because they met one of our requirements. The difference between believers and unbelievers will become more clear when we realize that only those who are called by God will come to Him; only when salvation is again considered as a work of God's sovereign grace will we appreciate its implications and transforming power.

We must teach believers that the Christian life has both privileges and responsibilities. Taking up our cross means just that: a willingness to suffer because we belong to Christ.

Specifically, we must expose the sin of the "me first" cult of individualism that has infected the church. We've read about the woman from a small Oklahoma congregation who took three elders to court for exercising church discipline against her. She objected to the idea of confessing her sin to the church. After winning the suit and receiving a financial settlement that was greater than the congregation's budget for six years, she declared, "I'm not saying I wasn't guilty. I was. But it was none of their business."

In this instance, submission to church leadership (Heb. 13:17) and the clear teaching that we should not take fellow believers to court (1 Cor. 6:1–8) were set aside in favor of personal interests. Her attorney remarked, "He was a single man. She was a single lady. And this is America." In other words, although obedience to church leaders may be laudable biblically, it is contrary to the American way of life.

How different this is from the spirit of Jesus, who pleased not Himself but made Himself of no reputation and was obedient to death (Rom. 15:3; Phil. 2:7–8). He did it for us, but more important, He did it for God.

We must also learn that selective obedience nullifies the authority of God. We've all been tempted to neglect church discipline for fear of criticism, a charge of inconsistency, or possibly a church split. But does our well-intended negligence further the work of Christ?

Under the guise of being relevant, loving, and broad-minded, we weaken the impact of the gospel. Little wonder that a member of a large evangelical church could tell me, "I can't remember the last time we've had someone saved."

As pastors, let's remember that we're not the ones who determine what we should preach, who can be remarried in our church, or what the structure of the home should be. It's not up to us to decide whether we should be selective in the television programs we watch, how much we should give, or whether we should witness to our neighbors. We are bondslaves of Jesus Christ, obligated to search Scripture to find an answer to the question, "Lord, what wilt thou have me to do?" (Acts 9:6 KJV).

George Gallup is optimistic. He believes that if properly nurtured, the new awareness of religion in America could bring more genuine converts into the church. But I fear that it won't happen as long as the distinction between the church and the world remains blurred. We've come a long way from the early church, when fear fell upon the multitudes and "none of the rest dared to associate with them" (Acts 5:13 NASB).

The millions who take their religion à la carte will someday discover they've had the wrong menu. Only those who pay the price of obedience can enjoy the nourishment of the bread from heaven.

It's not the people who claim to be Christians who will affect our country; it's those who accept the cost and live the Christian life.

# • 12 •

# Counseling

## *Must We Be Experts in Psychology?*

Is a pastor without psychological training qualified to counsel his flock, or must he limit himself to spiritual counseling and refer the more difficult cases to professionals?

Many Bible school graduates think they have to get a doctorate in psychology at a state university so they can become a counselor. They think they have to combine psychological training with their Bible school knowledge for maximum effectiveness. But psychologists and theologians dispute the extent to which psychological studies can successfully integrate with the Bible.

Personally, I am wary about attempts at integration. I find no biblical support to distinguish a spiritual problem from a psychological problem. At root, man's psychological problems, unless they are the result of physical or chemical causes, are spiritual—and where could we find a better analysis of man's need along with a supernatural remedy than in the Scriptures? Peter writes that our Lord's divine power has granted us "everything pertaining to life and godliness, through the true knowledge of Him who called us by His own glory and excellence" (2 Peter 1:3 NASB).

Paul writes, "For in Him all the fullness of Deity dwells in bodily form, and in Him you have been made complete, and He is the head over all rule and authority" (Col. 2:9–10). That leaves little room for using the techniques of secular psychology to help Christians achieve emotional and spiritual wholeness.

I am well aware that this matter of integration is more compli-
cated than it appears on the surface. It is easy to say that we should
use only the Bible and turn a deaf ear from everything psychology
would teach us. But, thanks to common grace, even those who do not
believe the Bible have occasionally hit upon biblical truths. So psychology may have some value in helping us understand man's predicament; it might provide some fodder for analysis. But its limitations
and potential for deception must be understood.

Larry Crabb, in his book *Effective Biblical Counseling*, advocates
that we "spoil the Egyptians"—we should use the insights, principles,
and techniques of psychology that are consistent with Scripture to
help us become more effective. I appreciate his desire to test the pre-
suppositions of secular theories so that we would accept only what is
biblical.[1]

Interestingly, in more recent writings, Crabb has concluded that
professional counselors often do not achieve the results attributed to
them. He believes that what broken people really need is the love
and support of the church, the body of Christ. When our physical
body has a wound, it has the power to heal itself; similarly, a healthy
church has the power to provide healing for its broken members.

Crabb says there must also be the humble recognition that some
members of the body will never be healed until they arrive in heaven.
Indeed, our first priority should never be having our emotional needs
met, but rather worshiping God. Thus, philosophies of counseling
often are wrongheaded; we must return to the conviction that our
desire for God must supersede our desire to be "fixed." In Crabb's
words, "Our agenda is to fix the world until it can properly take care
of us. God's agenda is to bring all things together in Christ until
every knee bows before Him."

And that, ultimately, is why we must be biblical in our counseling.
While secular theories might alleviate someone's pain and while
purely psychological insights might enable the hurting to cope, when
all is said and done, it is their relationship with God that really matters. A biblical counselor will always see beyond time to eternity.

Counseling is best described as accelerated discipleship. It is helping people apply God's solution their problems; it is a redirection of
their lives to that which will matter for all of eternity.

## A Biblical Approach

It's unfortunate that the expression "biblical counseling" has a negative connotation. Some people think it means that the antidote to every problem is just information, and that the relationship between the counselor and the counselee is therefore mechanistic and impersonal. Others see it as a simple philosophy that simply seeks to uncover hidden sins, and if these are confessed and forsaken all will be well.

A thoroughly biblical approach rejects such a simplistic notion. Paul stressed the personal dimension in exhortation and encouragement. He was a father to those who needed discipline and a mother to those who needed tender care (1 Thess. 2:7).

A familiar story from the Old Testament illustrates the point that often only godly insight can uncover the root cause of a problem and prescribe a cure. In Joshua 7, Israel lost thirty-six men when trying to conquer Ai. What would a secular analyst say about that ignominious defeat? That the army used the wrong strategy? That the weapons were outdated? That too few men were sent to the battle zone?

Incredibly, military matters had nothing to do with Israel's defeat. God said the reason was that a man had stolen some items and had hidden them in his tent (Josh. 7:10–12). One man's sin indicted others. God established a cause-effect relationship that defies scientific analysis. Secular man often fails to uncover the true nature of a problem because the cause may lie entirely outside his investigation. Spiritual causes are discovered only by those with scriptural insight into the ways of God and His dealings with men.

If I had been telling the story of Achan, I would have said, "Achan sinned." But God's commentary says, "The sons of Israel acted unfaithfully" (Josh. 7:1 NASB). Israel was a spiritual commonwealth bound together by a covenant.

A similar relationship exists between members of a family. "I, the Lord your God, am a jealous God, visiting the iniquity of the fathers on the children, on the third and the fourth generations of those who hate Me" (Exod. 20:5 NASB). When Ham acted indecently, his son Canaan was cursed (Gen. 9:25). Demons may harass a family line; hence, a child may be afflicted (Mark 9:20–21). In such cases, the influence of the parents and grandparents must be broken. Perhaps that is why the people of Israel confessed the sins of their fathers (Neh. 9:2).

Conversely, blessings may often be attributed to godly influences. The Lord shows "lovingkindness to thousands, to those who love Me and keep My commandments" (Exod. 20:6 NASB). Solomon was spared judgment because of his father David's sake (1 Kings 11:12). Laban was blessed because of Jacob (Gen. 30:27). And an unbelieving marriage partner is set apart for spiritual privileges because of a believing spouse (1 Cor. 7:14).

Concerning the body of Christ, Paul wrote, "If one member suffers, all the members suffer with it; if one member is honored, all the members rejoice with it" (1 Cor. 12:26 NASB). Here again we see that our lives are interrelated. We must recognize that one part of the body cannot suffer without the whole being affected. But, thankfully, it is also true that the more healthy the body, the more likely it is able to bring healing to its ailing members.

This solidarity helps us understand sin's consequences and cure more clearly. We will have a better understanding of how healing takes place.

A reflective knowledge of the Scriptures along with a compassionate heart can, under the guidance of the Spirit, be used to uncover the root cause of problems that elude a purely psychological approach. And what is important to remember is that there is not one right prescription for every problem.

## The Body Healing Itself

When a fellow believer falls into sin, part of the responsibility may be ours. If one member is spiritually cold, he lowers the temperature of everyone around him. If I stumble, I might bring you down with me. We are united in our failures.

Spiritual power is unleashed when the church diffuses its strength throughout the whole body. Believers overcome depression, forgive abusive parents, and develop wholesome self-images when the body provides love and acceptance. Fractured personalities can be put back together within the context of people who see another's needs as being their own.

No one counsels with a sense of detachment when he realizes that failure is a shared experience. When a family breaks up, we all hurt. My first response to a believer's defeat should be to search my own heart.

Such an understanding of Scripture does not absolve individuals of responsibility. We are not programmed by the performances of others. God has tempered parental influence with personal responsibility (Ezek. 18:20).

The church family owes a huge debt to God because of our disobedience; we bear the burden of our sins both corporately and individually. The warriors who went to capture Ai would have had a greater concern for Achan's spiritual life if they had remembered that his actions were bound up with theirs.

Personal sin is also interrelated. The works of the flesh come in clusters. We cannot tolerate sin in one part of our life and be experiencing victory in another. If we close one room of our life to God, darkness settles over the whole house.

One man who struggled with pornography could not overcome his secret sin until he made restoration for items he had stolen many years ago. Another man overcame cigarette smoking after he asked his parents to forgive him for the rebellion of his youth, accepting responsibility for the days when he had begun the habit against their wishes.

In marriage counseling, I've sometimes asked a couple if they had premarital sex. "What difference does that make?" they retort. But if they have, they've planted seeds that have borne bitter fruit. They've forgotten that you never reap in the same season that you sow.

Sin sprouts roots in any number of unpredictable directions. If covetousness can lead to the defeat of an army, might not cheating on one's income tax lead to excessive anger or even immorality? James says, "A double minded man is unstable in all his ways" (James 1:8 KJV).

This knowledge of sin's effects ought to influence our counseling. We must see failure in its larger context and take time for spiritual inventory.

How might we have failed our brothers and sisters in Christ? What hidden sins within a family or church might have provided the climate for marital strife, moral sin, or emotional turbulence? I must ask God to search my heart and then seek His wisdom to identify the cause of personal and corporate defeat.

I believe that if Joshua had come to God before he sent men to Ai, the Lord would have revealed Achan's secret sin, and Israel would have been spared defeat. But Joshua acted hastily. Even on a later occasion, he got into trouble by not seeking the counsel of the Lord (Josh. 9).

When unconfessed sin is found, it must be judged. Achan and his family were stoned and then burned (Josh. 7:25). A heap of stones was left in the Valley of Achor as a memorial of that shameful event, and "the Lord turned from the fierceness of His anger" (v. 26 NASB).

But often God does judge us as individuals and as churches because we have been unwilling to make a thorough housecleaning of our lives. The Holy Spirit is willing to search our hearts when we become honest (Ps. 139:23–24).

*Achor* means "trouble," an apparent reference to the severe judgment that Achan and his family received there. But hundreds of years later, the prophet Hosea said that the Valley of Achor will be a door of hope (Hos. 2:15). Hidden sin becomes a place of judgment; when sin is confessed and forsaken, however, that place becomes a door of hope. Once sin was put away, Joshua and his men defeated Ai, apparently without the loss of a single soldier. When sin is judged, blessing flows.

Every pastor must be comfortable with his own philosophy of counseling, but I suspect that we'd all be more successful if we sought God's wisdom in uncovering the causes of spiritual failure. God wants to build a monument of victory in the valley of defeat, and He's given us the tools to help Him.

Let no one say that my theory of counseling is simply to hunt for hidden sin. In some instances, the cause may be sin in general; no specific sin needs to be confessed.

I've learned several very important lessons in counseling. First, we cannot expect to have the same approach to every problem. Sometimes, we must try to uncover sin; at other times, we must simply give love and support. An abused child, for example, needs unconditional love and acceptance. His emotional problems likely will not be helped by trying to uncover hidden sins, though forgiveness toward his parents will become necessary at some point.

I feel sorry for counselors who think that everyone needs the same approach, the same analysis, and the same truth. Each person is different; each needs an individualized approach. Not everyone suffers from rejection. Not everyone who is depressed is struggling with anger. Not everyone is helped by telling them that they just must "obey God" and all will be well.

Second, though my counseling experiences are limited, I have seen the best results through persistent, believing prayer. I spend a good chunk of time praying for my counselee as well as having him or her pray according to my direction. I am a firm believer in the promise that God not only gives us wisdom but also pours healing into the lives of all who earnestly seek Him. "He heals the broken-hearted, and binds up their wounds" (Ps. 147:3 NASB).

We don't need to be experts in psychology to be effective counselors. We just need to be scripturally sound and emotionally sensitive to enter into the needs of our people. Our faith is not in ourselves but in the "Wonderful Counselor" who will hear our prayers as we call upon Him.

## · 13 ·

# Worship

## *Can It Happen in a Structured Service?*

As a new bride, a woman in a remote village dreamed about the security and happiness her marriage would bring. Perhaps her expectations were unrealistic. Maybe she was too preoccupied with her own ambitions to recognize the first signs of tension in her marriage.

But the tensions mushroomed. Eventually she and her husband agreed they could no longer live together. The decision was agonizing but from all appearances necessary. They were divorced.

Time heals all wounds, or at least lessens the pain. After the woman had pulled herself together emotionally, she met a man who seemed to have all the qualities her first husband lacked. This marriage would be a success, she thought.

When her second marriage showed signs of strain, the woman dared not let herself think it would end like the first. Yet, the foundations of that relationship began to crumble. Before long, the woman experienced a second divorce.

Some women would have buried their frustrations in a career. They would have relocated in another city, gone back to school, or learned a skill. But this woman could not. Her family believed not only that a woman's place is at home but also that she is to be obedient to the whims of her husband. Furthermore, in her locality, no jobs were available to women. All she knew—all she *could* know—were household chores, the drudgery of routine.

Her decision to marry the third time was easier to make. By that time, the woman was bitter at God and disgruntled with men. If her marriage didn't work, another divorce would rescue her from the bonds of meaningless vows. Predictably, she experienced a third divorce. Then a fourth and a fifth.

When she met another man, she decided not to bother with the formality of a wedding. They just lived together under common law.

And then she met Jesus Christ, who offered her living water. He also invited her to worship the Most High God. "Our fathers worshiped in this mountain," she offered (John 4:20 NASB). "Woman, believe Me," Christ replied, "an hour is coming when neither in this mountain, nor in Jerusalem, shall you worship the Father. . . . But an hour is coming, and now is, when the true worshipers shall worship the Father in spirit and truth; for such people the Father seeks to be His worshipers" (John 4:21, 23 NASB). Christ extended an invitation for her to become a worshiper, and through her, the invitation is given to us all.

### The Essence of Worship

"To worship," said William Temple, Archbishop of Canterbury from 1942 to 1944, "is to quicken the conscience by the holiness of God, to feed the mind with the truth of God, to purge the imagination by the beauty of God, to open the heart to the love of God, and to devote the will to the purpose of God."[1]

The woman at the well considered worship a matter of outward conformity. But Christ taught that it was a matter of spirit and truth. The Jews worshiped in Jerusalem, the Samaritans on Mount Gerizim. From that time, worship would not be confined to geography. It was no longer a matter of being in the temple or on the right hilltop.

How often we assume that we must be in church to worship. We are told that the church building is "God's house," but that can be misleading. In the Old Testament, God dwelt in the temple; His glory settled within the holy of holies. But God was displeased with the temple worship in Jerusalem. He is equally unimpressed with our cathedral worship today.

Today the holy of holies resides in the body of every believer. Worship can take place anywhere; we are always in God's presence, and He is available for our adoration. Worship isn't just listening to a sermon, appreciating choir music, or joining to sing hymns. In fact, it isn't even necessarily prayer, for prayer sometimes comes from an unbroken, unyielded heart. Worship is not an external activity precipitated by the right environment. To worship in spirit is to draw near to God with an undivided heart. We must come in full agreement without hiding anything or disregarding His will.

Augustine spoke of those who have tried unsuccessfully to find God. "They were probably inflated by their pride of learning and so were misled into seeking Him by throwing out their chests rather than beating upon their breasts."

In worship, our hunger for God is both satisfied and increased. In His presence, we desire "all the fullness of God" and we want to be done with sin, we want the church purified, and we long for the return of Christ. We are even homesick for heaven.

## Leading Others to Worship

How can we as pastors help our people worship? First, we must stress that worship demands preparation. People cannot worship in church if they have not met the Lord before arriving at the door. The sixty minutes before Sunday school and church is, for many Christians, the most unholy hour of the week. Eating, dressing, and scurrying around the house to finish those last-minute tasks and then driving to church out-of-sorts with one another is not conducive to a prepared heart. What we do *before* the service will determine what happens *within* the service.

The form of worship is not as important as the spiritual condition of the human heart. John MacArthur Jr. wrote in *The Ultimate Priority*, "If our corporate worship isn't the expression of our individual worshiping lives, it is unacceptable. If you think you can live any way you want and then go to church on Sunday morning and turn on worship with the saints, you're wrong."[2]

David said, "Unite my heart to fear Thy name" (Ps. 86:11 NASB). Our congregations must also come to God single-mindedly, in full agreement. We dare not think worship takes place automatically because we are all in the same place.

Second, we must worship in truth. Worship is not just an emotional exercise but a response of the heart built on truth about God. "The Lord is near to all who call upon Him, To all who call upon Him in truth" (Ps. 145:18 NASB). Worship that is not based on God's Word is but an emotional encounter with oneself.

Do you remember what happened when Nehemiah asked Ezra to read the scrolls of Scripture? "Then Ezra blessed the Lord the great God. And all the people answered, 'Amen, amen!' while lifting up their hands; then they bowed low and worshiped the Lord with their faces to the ground" (Neh. 8:6 NASB). The truth of God in their minds led the Israelites to bow their knees in worship.

In his book *Between Two Worlds*, John Stott says, "Word and worship belong indissolubly to each other. All worship is an intelligent and loving response to the revelation of God, because it is the adoration of His name. Therefore, acceptable worship is impossible without preaching. For preaching is making known the name of the Lord, and worship is praising the name of the Lord made known."[3]

There can be no worship without obedience to truth. That's why worship often involves sacrifice. It's not just praising God but praising Him through our instant response to His requests. When Abraham was asked to sacrifice Isaac, he said to his young men, "Stay here with the donkey, and I and the lad will go yonder; and we will worship and return to you" (Gen. 22:5 NASB). Abraham expected to slay his son; yet, he called that worship. Worship is wanting God more than the life of a son. And we cannot worship in church unless we have made some hard choices for God during the week. To speak of worship without surrender is like expecting an airplane to fly with one wing.

The people in Isaiah's day were not condemned because they sang the wrong songs. God did not judge them because they prayed unorthodox prayers. The nation even brought sacrifices. But they lacked surrendered hearts. Christ, quoting Isaiah, said,

"You hypocrites, rightly did Isaiah prophesy of you, saying,
'This people honors Me with their lips,
But their heart is far away from Me.
But in vain do they worship Me,
Teaching as their doctrines the precepts of men.'"
(Matt. 15:7–9 NASB)

Talk is cheap. It's obedience to truth that really matters. That's why worship is always costly. It means we come before God with a signed blank check.

Finally, Christ said that worship is a matter of priority. "Such people the Father seeks to be His worshipers" (John 4:23 NASB). At first glance, that statement seems odd. Would not all people, especially Christians, want to worship the Father? Would it not be natural for us, the creatures, to want to meet our Creator? Yet, it's Almighty God who does the seeking. My guess is that relatively few people respond.

How can we entice our people to take God up on His offer? For one thing, we must be worshipers ourselves. If we don't schedule time to worship God with meaning, we can't expect our congregations to do it either. Ann Ortlund wrote, "A congregation doesn't become broken because the minister tells them to. They get broken when he gets broken."

Second, we must concentrate on sharing with our people the glories of who God is. We should let them know that the Christian life is more than seeking freedom from sin.

Christians must also long to draw closer to God. If we are quenching our thirst at forbidden fountains, we have no reason to expect God to be satisfying. If we are not nourished by the bread from heaven, we will satiate ourselves with crumbs from the world. Once we have become addicted to the world's nourishment, our appetite for God is spoiled.

How can this apply to next Sunday morning? Pastors are not actors performing on stage for a crowd of staid bystanders. Rather, the whole congregation must participate while God, our audience, watches to see how well we do. He's monitoring us to find those whose hearts are perfect toward Him.

Let's begin by asking: How can we lift our congregations into God's presence and leave them there to cry, praise, and enjoy? Do we emphasize that they are actually on stage before God? Is there planned spontaneity, where the Lord is free to do something not listed in the bulletin?

God gave the privilege of worship to an immoral woman. Regardless of her past failures, worship was an exciting possibility. He now extends the same invitation to us. RSVP.

## • 14 •

# Public Invitations

*Are We Being Misunderstood?*

"Those who want to accept Christ as Savior, please leave your seats and come and stand at the front of the platform."

Most of us have heard invitations like that ever since we were children. And if we were shy, we might conclude that we simply cannot be saved.

In some churches, abandoning the invitation would be considered the first step toward liberalism. Even those who think that "coming forward" has no biblical support still practice regular public invitations and would never dream of changing them.

In the minds of many, having people come forward proves that the pastor is evangelistic and that God is at work. Regardless of what happens in the counseling room, the fact that there has been an outward sign gives the congregation the feeling that the church is on the move.

But this past summer, as I sat on a park bench and heard a young preacher urge people to come forward to receive Christ, I realized once again our urgent need to rethink our method of giving invitations. No matter how accustomed to them we may be, we must subject our practice to vigorous biblical scrutiny.

Charles Finney was among the first evangelists to call people forward during a service. He defended the practice by saying it served the same purpose as baptism in the days of the apostles. But he was putting the cart before the horse; baptism is a sign that one has been converted, not a prerequisite for conversion. Ever since Finney's time, public invitations have generated similar misunderstandings.

In some churches, walking forward and "coming to Christ" are linked to the point that people are led to believe one action can't happen without the other. To come forward is to "come to Jesus."

What happens when we link these two separate acts? Basically, it perpetuates the notion that walking before a crowd has some special merit in the conversion process. Those who are afraid to go forward may actually think they cannot be saved.

When I was ten years old, I was too embarrassed to walk in front of several hundred people. So I suffered through those invitations in which we sang all the stanzas of a hymn half a dozen times. Meanwhile, I was thinking, "If I have to go forward in front of all these people, I'll just have to go to hell."

More recently, I attended a meeting where the evangelist said, "Come, run to Christ!" A couple got up and ran forward, and he said, "See this couple! Others of you should get up and *run* to Christ!" I felt sorry for people with physical disabilities who wouldn't even be able to "walk to Christ," much less *run*! Yes, there are people who think they can be saved only when they go forward in a meeting and register their "decision" for Christ.

Perhaps there is a reason why a major denomination in the United States disclosed that, in a specified year, they had recorded 294,784 "decisions for Christ." But they could find only 14,337 in fellowship. Yet, the process of recording these great numbers continues without anyone asking what has gone wrong.

D. L. Moody, bless him, refused to count the number of decisions because he knew that many of them were not genuinely converted. Our numbers and God's numbers are just not one and the same. Perhaps not even close.

## Misconceptions About Invitations

Although evangelists privately admit that a person can be saved without going forward, many of them do not want the word to get around. Saying, "Why don't you leave your seat and come to receive Christ?" is carefully calculated to urge people to respond physically to their appeal.

One evangelist obscures the issues even more by saying he wants to make it hard for people to respond to Christ. He derides this generation's "easy believism"; he wants to make faith tough. For him, the place to begin is by walking forward in front of the whole congregation. Taking Christ's invitation to discipleship as an invitation to salvation, he insists that people walk forward publicly to be saved. Another preacher says he wants to give people an opportunity to "demonstrate" for Jesus Christ: "People are demonstrating for everything today; why don't you get out of your seat and demonstrate for Christ?" He thought he was making it difficult to become a Christian, but actually he was making it easy. There is nothing repulsive to the flesh about demonstrating for a worthy cause. Little wonder that when a counselor asked a young man why he had come forward his unhesitating reply was, "Because the world's in a mess, and I want to help."

Yes, it is difficult to become a Christian. But the difficulty is in acknowledging our sin and helplessness—precisely what proud hearts are unwilling to do. It's hard to admit that we must cast ourselves on the mercy of God in Jesus Christ. The difficulty is with the blindness of the human heart and an unwillingness to see our own condition before God.

Many people who pray to be saved are unchanged simply because they have not understood the seriousness of their condition and why their trust must be transferred to Christ alone. They consider "receiving Christ" as one more good thing to do, like attending mass or praying the Lord's Prayer. They are glad to recite a prayer but quite unwilling to acknowledge their utter helplessness in God's holy presence.

Making it appear as if walking forward is the hard part and necessary for salvation contributes to people's confusion about the gospel. It mixes faith and works and gives the impression that being willing to come forward is somehow related to being willing to "come to Christ" a phrase that means different things to different people.

I cringed when I heard a person who attends a church that gives such invitations say, "I want to be saved, but I'll have to wait until next Sunday." This popular misconception about invitations not only adds the requirement of works to the gospel but also puts assurance on a wrong foundation. Many people today think they are saved because they have gone forward to "receive Christ."

Somehow, the natural man thinks that if he hasn't performed a saving act, he has at least contributed to it by walking forward. Because of his heart's blindness and deception, he thinks he must do the best he can to repair his relationship with God. And afterward he prides himself in having had the courage to do so.

I've often heard a Christian who should know better say, "Wasn't it great to see three people saved this morning?" Because three people went forward during the invitation, he assumed that regeneration had taken place. But someone can go forward, pray an appropriate prayer, and still leave unconverted.

Yet, this style of invitation is sometimes defended because it makes good psychology: people should make some kind of response to "nail down" their decision. That phrase sounds reasonable, but it breeds confusion. Those who haven't gone forward may think they cannot be saved, and those who have gone forward think they are saved because of their courageous act of walking in front of several hundred people.

Dr. Lewis Sperry Chafer, founder of Dallas Theological Seminary, frequently gave public invitations in the early years of his ministry. But he eventually concluded that they obscured the issues of the gospel. He said, "Careful students of evangelism have noticed that where the necessity of public action as a part of conversion has been most emphasized there has been a corresponding increase in the God-dishonoring record of so-called 'backsliding'; and this is natural."[1]

The reason is obvious. Unconverted people think they are saved simply because they came forward. They feel better after they have done something.

In the New Testament, some people believed on Christ while He was teaching. Let's not think that the Holy Spirit converts people only when they respond to a public invitation. I'm glad I discovered that I could be saved in my own home, on my knees in a sparse farm living room. Let us make it our supreme task to urge men and women to believe in our mighty, omnipresent Christ.

I realize, however, that many have received Christ as Savior when they responded to an altar call. Some even say that deciding to walk forward was a test of their sincerity in surrendering to the Holy Spirit's conviction. But we should never give the impression that the new birth and walking forward are inseparably linked.

## A Balanced Approach

God's part in salvation is to convict the sinner, draw him, and grant him the gift of repentance. All man can do is respond to what God is doing and cast himself upon God's mercy that he might be saved. To associate that step closely with the act of coming forward in a meeting is to dilute the purity of the gospel and to focus on the wrong issue.

It's not whether a man is willing to walk in front of other people that is important to God. It's whether he is willing to acknowledge his sin and receive the mercy that God extends to him through the Cross.

As Chafer said, "The one necessary step—the acceptance of Christ as Savior—can be performed only in the secret of the heart itself, by a personal choice and action of the will. This is a dealing with Christ alone, and as the time of this decision is the most critical moment in a human life, reason demands that it should be guarded from every distracting and confusing condition."[2]

Giving a public invitation to the unconverted has also led to the embarrassment of large numbers of apparent converts coming forward and then failing to show spiritual fruit in their lives. We could be spared this questioning of the power of the gospel if we waited for the fruit of repentance, rather than counting converts based on the outward sign of walking forward.

Of course, the need to give an invitation is urgent; but it must always be an invitation to come to Christ, not to the evangelist or to the front of the platform. Whenever possible—publicly or privately— we should urge men and women to repentance and faith. We must not let them think that they can add to the work that Christ has already done.

After all I have said, you might be surprised to hear me say that there is a place for invitations, as long as they are not directly associated with accepting Christ as Savior. It is appropriate to give Christians an opportunity to confess Christ or to invite people to receive spiritual counsel.

Paul wrote, "If you confess with your mouth Jesus as Lord, and believe in your heart that God raised Him from the dead, you shall be saved; for with the heart man believes, resulting in righteousness, and with the mouth he confesses, resulting in salvation" (Rom. 10:9–10 NASB).

But that passage cannot be interpreted to mean that regeneration comes about by a public confession. Such an understanding would disagree with scores of other passages. Verse 9 must be interpreted in the light of verse 10. How is a right standing gained before God? "For with the heart man believeth unto righteousness" (v. 10 KJV). It is in the heart that the will exercised by the Holy Spirit responds to the saving work of Christ. The confession "unto salvation" is a result of having received the gift of righteousness. Thus, the believer testifies with his mouth to what God has wrought in his heart.

So we could invite new converts to share their decision with the pastor, a counselor, or the whole congregation. In effect, this "confession" could be a testimony of God's saving grace. It also would be the opportunity to receive further counsel. With such invitations God is well pleased.

We could also make an effort to separate the physical response from the spiritual act of conversion. At Moody Church, I invite people to the front so they can discuss a spiritual need with a member of the pastoral staff or a counselor, providing an opportunity to pray, ask questions, and receive counsel—whether one is saved or unsaved.

Let's not associate the act of walking forward with "coming to Christ," and let's not be afraid to tell people that they can be saved where they are seated—or wherever they might find themselves next week—to tell them that they should go home and seek God, preferably on their knees, that they might come to the assurance of faith. They don't have to wait until next Sunday.

If, after considering this matter, you still believe that you must give an invitation that urges the unconverted to come forward, I beg you to be honest, clear, and simple. You and I have heard evangelists say, "Just raise your hand," and the sinner thinks that that act is the end of the matter. But then, suddenly, he is told to "come forward," which he never intended to do. In extreme cases, I have actually been present when preachers have pointed out those who have raised their hands. One even said, "The man with the blue shirt . . ." That kind of gimmickry is surely unworthy of the gospel. Let us not be surprised when some people who have been embarrassed leave the church and never return.

Yes, let us urge people to come to Christ—not to the preacher, the platform, or even a counselor—but to the invisible Christ. Only a clear invitation is worthy of a clear gospel.

# • 15 •

# God's Judgment

## *How Can We Recognize It Today?*

At a recent meeting of religious leaders, one respected observer of the American political scene remarked, "We've lost the abortion battle in Washington. Now there's no turning back . . . ; we are sliding toward the judgment of God."

I'm not qualified to say that the fight against abortion is dead politically, nor can I put a timetable on God's judgment. But we cannot escape the consequences of killing four thousand unborn babies every day.

Of course, America is inflicted with many other ills: violent crime, divorce, teen suicide, and a sharp increase in illegitimate births. As William J. Bennet has pointed out, no matter how much the government spends on pathologies, the situation is only becoming worse. "Many of the most serious social and behavioral problems we now face (particularly among our young)," he states, "are remarkably resistant to government cures."

It's popular to blame the Supreme Court, the humanists, and the radical feminists. To be sure, they have contributed to the liberalization of America. But if God is using them to judge us, might not the responsibility more properly be laid at the feet of those who know the living God but who have failed to influence society?

If we were few in number, we could more easily evade censure. But there are tens of thousands of evangelical pastors in America who lead several million born-again believers. Yet, we're losing one battle after another. Perhaps the church doesn't suffer for the sins of the world as much as the world suffers for the sins of the church. Because of our cowardly silence in the midst of abortion, pornography, and the erosion of our religious liberties, and because of our acceptance of compromise within the church, the salt has lost its savor and the light flickers. In our desperation, we look for solutions to stem the tide; we want to have someone rise up and fight our battles for us.

Perhaps the answer we seek is close at hand, but we have been confused regarding our agenda. We have failed to be the church at a time when our nation needs to see righteous examples of leadership and hope. We are indeed under God's judgment as a nation, but perhaps we are unaware of it. The matter is worthy of careful thought.

### Where Have We Failed?

First, we have neglected the unconverted. We give our lives to an evangelical subculture that is known to many only by the caricatures of the media. Unfortunately, the message that means most to us is often lost simply because we have been unwilling to share the gospel backed by a credible lifestyle.

If each Christian family actively witnessed and discipled those who come to Christ (we expect much more from our missionaries), our impact among the unconverted would be phenomenal. Yet we are told that 95 percent of all Christians have never given a clear witness to an unsaved neighbor. However much we may talk about the power of the gospel, we are apparently afraid to share it. At root is our reluctance to believe that the gospel is actually "the power of God unto salvation" (Rom. 1:16 KJV).

Second, we have retreated behind what Francis Schaeffer calls "false pietism" in regard to social issues. We have eschewed anything that necessitates sacrificial involvement. We've neglected to "do good unto all men, especially unto them who are of the household of faith" (Gal. 6:10 KJV). As long as we live well, can choose our friends, and are assured a comfortable retirement, we don't care too much about newspaper headlines. What matters is that our personal peace and affluence not be disrupted.

Of course, we may preach an occasional sermon against abortion, but are we willing to help teenage girls who are pregnant? We may condemn injustice, but are we willing to use our own finances and influences to help those who have been treated unfairly? Talk is cheap. It's easy to say the right words and then hope that someone else will fight our battles.

Also, we have accepted the world's values in entertainment, leisure, and success. We have lost our ability to critique society. Since the church is so often indistinguishable from the world, the unconverted have no model of righteousness.

Every Christian couple that divorces causes others to question the power of God. When a church splits over trivial matters, it says to the community that God cannot bring restoration and forgiveness to His people. When fathers neglect to lead their families in prayer and Bible instruction, they subtly give the impression that God's counsel is optional! And when we are willing to rationalize sensuality, selfishness, and greed, we are, in effect, admitting that Christ is unable to free us from sin. As a result, we have nothing to say to this generation.

In desperation, we have turned to politics, believing that if only we had the right leaders we would turn this nation around. We have forgotten that if there is any good news it will never come from Washington but rather from the people of God who can point others to Christ.

### What Form Will God's Judgment Take?

During the cold war era, we often imagined that judgment would come in the form of war with Russia. We expected a nuclear holocaust that would wipe us off the map. We thought we ourselves might be enslaved to Communism during the days when its leaders assured us that they would rule the world.

Today, some people think that the judgment will come in a famine, an earthquake, or killer tornadoes. Yes, these are the judgment of God, given by Him to remind us that we all must die and that it is a fearful thing to fall into God's hands. Although these judgments fall on the just and the unjust, they are a picture of God's future judgment. The earth is corrupt, and more corruption will follow.

Yet, there is another form of judgment more closely tied to the cause-effect relationships of sin. After God warned the Israelites of famines, wars, and boils, He predicted that the final judgment would be captivity. "Your sons and your daughters shall be given to another people, while your eyes shall look on and yearn for them continually; but there shall be nothing you can do" (Deut. 28:32 NASB). The severest judgment was the scattering of Israel's families.

Though in a different way, the same thing is happening to us today. One-half of all children born this year will, at some time, live with only one parent. As our homes continue to break up, depression, hatred, and child abuse result. Such consequences of disobedience will escalate.

Or perhaps God's judgment will include intensifying emotional disorders. He told the Israelites that their disobedience would bring "despair of soul" (Deut. 28:65 NASB). Unresolved guilt surfaces under different labels—anger, insensitivity, depression. With millions of women having abortions and an equal or even greater number of men guilty of sexual immorality, future generations will find mental illness on the increase. We can expect our nation to rot from within.

### What Can We Do?

The only hope for America can be found in the church. The body of Christ still wields awesome power. If we are brought to our knees, and if we are willing to pay the price of obedience, God may begin to give us spiritual victories that could stem abortion, infanticide, and drug abuse. Perhaps, in His grace, He might even be pleased to send us a spiritual awakening.

When Mordecai told Esther that she should go before the king to intercede for the Jews, she hesitated, fearing for her own life. But Mordecai replied, "Do not imagine that you in the king's palace can escape any more than all the Jews. . . . And who knows whether you have not attained royalty for such a time as this?" (Esther 4:13–14 NASB).

Esther had to be willing to lay her life on the line before deliverance would come. She couldn't feel content because of her own supposed security. In the end, it wasn't the rooms of an opulent palace but only God who could save her. So she risked her life, saying, "If I perish, I perish" (v. 16). Only at such cost did God bring deliverance. Though Esther and the Jews were a minority, that mattered little when God took up their cause.

Our political options in fighting matters such as abortion, the expansion of homosexual rights and the disintegration of TV entertainment appear to be limited, but that is not a cause for discouragement. What the Supreme Court thinks is meaningless when God fights on behalf of His people.

Perhaps God is trying to teach us that we cannot depend on human agencies to turn this nation back to Him. We must wait before Him until He gives us the grace to weep for our nation and its leaders. We must repent of our comfortable relationship with the world. We must grieve not so much for ungodly men who make unjust laws but for the people of God who are spiritually paralyzed and unable to witness to Christ's power in every sphere of life.

God is willing to meet us, but, even at this late hour, I'm not sure that we are ready to pay the price.

If we are as desperate as we profess to be, I propose that we as pastors

- lead our congregations by example in witnessing, community involvement, and teaching
- spend one day a week in prayer and fasting for ourselves, our churches, and our nation
- stand with our families in their desire to represent Christ in their schools and their vocations
- refuse to buy into the present culture of sensuality, individualism, and greed
- teach our people how to defend their faith in our pluralistic world

Our time is short. Our political and legal options are beginning to close. We are on the way down. Only God can save us now.

# A Kinder, Gentler Theology

## *Is It Biblical or Cultural?*

Listen to some evangelicals and you'll be led to believe that man does not exist for God's benefit but that God exists for man's benefit. Man tells God when he wants to be saved, how rich he'd like to become, and even his own version of theology.

The clay is giving the Potter instructions.

We've been seeing trends in this direction for some time. Many evangelicals have left the Reformation doctrines of total depravity, the bondage of the human will, and man's need for sovereign grace. A general commitment to Christ substitutes for repentance, and emotional feelings replace worship.

I agree with Joe Bayly, who wrote, "In our 'let's give God a hand' (applaud, everyone) Christian culture, we have lost a sense of wonder, of awe, of approaching an Almighty God when we pray. Even our worship is narcissistic."

A spirit of accommodation permeates the evangelical pulpits of our land. Sometimes obvious, sometimes subtle, but always dangerous, much preaching today is shaped by the culture of our times. The Bible is bent to accommodate culture rather than to change it.

### A New Theology

I don't know when these trends received their greatest impetus, but I know that Robert Schuller articulated a man-centered approach to evangelical theology in his book *Self-Esteem—The New Reformation.* Although it was appropriate for Calvin and Luther to think theocentrically, because in their day everyone was in the church, Schuller says times have changed: "What we need is a theology of salvation that begins and ends with a recognition of every person's hunger for glory."[1]

Sin, traditionally thought to be against God, is now defined as against man: "any act or thought that robs myself or another human being of his or her self-esteem."[2]

The differences between the sixteenth-century Reformation and this new reformation are obvious. Gone is the idea that a knowledge of God is one's highest goal; a knowledge of ourselves and of our need for self-respect is now the first item on the theological agenda. God is not so much a judge who has been offended as He is a servant who is waiting to affirm our dignity. We come to Him on the basis of our self-worth rather than the blood of Christ.

How, then, shall we present this gospel? Schuller says that Christ never called anyone a sinner. "The Gospel message is not only faulty, but potentially dangerous if it has to put a person down before it attempts to lift him up,"[3] he says. In effect, we stand before God to be exalted, not to be abased.

This reformation, then, is basically a call to a new preoccupation with ourselves rather than with God. But, unfortunately, as man is lifted up, God is dethroned.

Let's not think, however, that Schuller's book is an isolated case of Christian humanism. The fact that some so-called evangelicals accept this new reformation is proof enough that man-centered theology has permeated high places. I'm afraid that all of us have been affected.

The outworking of such a view of theology can be seen in how some ministers have accepted Evangelical Feminism in which great erudition is used to set aside the clear biblical teaching concerning male leadership in our homes and churches. There is little doubt that many arguments for egalitarianism are much more dependent on the spirit of our age than on Scripture.

Radical Armenianism, with its emphasis on free will and the unbiblical notion that not even God knows the future (hence, not even He knows who are the elect!), is little more than an accommodation to the man-centered theology of the age. One minister in an evangelical denomination, true to the Armenianism of the day, read John 3:16 from his pulpit this way: "God so loved the world that He *bet* His only begotten Son that whosoever believeth in Him should not perish . . ." (emphasis added). He said that Christ might have died and without saving anyone; God just took a risk and had no idea whether anyone would believe.

It's regrettable that the church leadership did not rise up to censure him. I would like to think that even older Armenians would have agreed that he was preaching heresy. But there is a new wind blowing, and many evangelicals are setting their sails to catch the breeze. God is being refashioned, made into our own image.

## The Consequences

What are the consequences of such thinking? First, theology itself becomes relative. To a greater or lesser extent, theology itself is based on the opinion poll. Men such as Schuller know that people want to hear something positive, so they give it to them. A pastor in one of America's largest and most innovative churches says that he cannot preach on holiness because no one is interested. To reach the unchurched, all messages must conform to this basic dictum: Help them see the immediate benefit Christianity can be to them.

Can you imagine Isaiah asking the people of Judah what they'd like to hear before he prepared his sermon? Or Christ tailoring His message to suit the Pharisees' hunger for personal glory?

It's easy to recognize the extremes, but we as pastors also ought to plead guilty to preaching what is popular rather than what is true. We sometimes skirt church discipline, the biblical standards for church leadership, and the Scriptures' denunciation of materialism for fear of rocking the ecclesiastical boat. Why alienate those who pay your salary? A bugle call is an unwelcome irritation to those at ease in Zion.

Many pastors who would die for the doctrine of the infallibility of Scripture never preach on the doctrine of hell. Indeed, many pastors who profess allegiance to the Scriptures no longer believe in eternal punishment but have adopted the theory of annihilation; they believe that the unconverted will be thrown into the flames and consumed. Apparently, this kinder, gentler punishment is not based on a careful rethinking of Scripture but on our natural abhorrence of the doctrine of hell.

How easy it is to exchange "Thus saith the Lord" for "Thus saith psychology," or "Thus saith the church board," or even "Thus saith society." Pastors are called by God to stand apart from society, to preach the Word of God regardless of whether it's what people want to hear. God's absolute justice, mercy, and love, along with Christ's substitutionary atonement, can never be compromised to accommodate current psychology. We can't criticize the world's relativism if we have a relativism of our own. Good preaching brings together the turbulent predicament of man and the unchangeable grace of God.

Second, man-centered theology leads to incomplete repentance. What is the basis on which we approach God, our inherent value as persons, or Christ's sacrifice on the cross?

For the Christian humanist, man's sin is not so much an offense to God as it is an offense to man. Because we are valuable unconditionally, God is waiting to accept us. The assumption is that He owes us something; we do not come as undeserving but as deserving sinners.

How different is the teaching of the Bible. Yes, we have dignity as persons; but, because we are corrupt, God owes us nothing. If we get what we deserve, we'll be in hell forever. So we come in humility, recognizing that whatever God gives us is a gift—an undeserved favor. And the basis of our coming is the blood of Christ, not our value as persons.

I've found that incomplete repentance often leads to resentment against God. The logic is obvious: If He exists for my benefit, what happens when my "hunger for glory" remains unsatisfied? Why does God not come to my aid to help me become the fulfilled human being I desire to be?

Humans are notorious for insisting on their "rights." If we don't see ourselves as undeserving sinners, we'll be upset when God doesn't do what we think He ought. Ultimately, those who are willing to bow under God's sovereignty are those who are satisfied.

Initially, Job felt that God owed him blessings. He believed that if he served God faithfully, blessings ought to follow. When tragedy came, his wife suggested, "Curse God and die!" (Job 2:9 NASB). She thought that God owed her happiness. If He did not come through for them, so be it.

But at the end of the book, Job came to full repentance. God owed him nothing—not even an explanation for his suffering. When he saw God, he abhorred himself and said, "I repent in dust and ashes" (Job 42:6 NASB).

No one repents unless he sees himself as undeserving. If I am worthy of God's blessing, grace is diminished. It's His acceptance of us despite our corruption that magnifies His grace. We are not doing our parishioners a favor by exalting them at the expense of God.

Third, our watered down theology dilutes our impact in society. We all know about the resurgence of evangelicalism in the last twenty years, but our influence is not being widely felt. As I have mentioned elsewhere in this book, religion is up, but morality is down.

Recently, I heard a report that the TV viewing habits of Christians and non-Christians are practically indistinguishable. New attempts to rate TV programs and provide incentives for better viewing content have largely failed. In our desire to be heard by the world, we have lost our motivation to be separate from it. Our witness for Christ has a hollow ring.

Might not our impotency be traced to an exaggerated view of man's ability to the detriment of God's sovereignty? One reason Jonathan Edwards and George Whitefield had such widespread influence is because they insisted that the human heart is in a state of total corruption apart from the gracious intervention of God.

Such preaching confronted men and women with their needs. Sinners cried to God for mercy that they might not be consumed by His wrath. Conversion was not a decision made leisurely, but people sought God "to make [their] calling and election sure" (2 Peter 1:10 KJV).

Someone has said that the marks of a strong church are wet eyes, bent knees, and a broken heart. We'll never be powerful until we let God be God and jealously guard His honor.

## Our Responsibility

How can we stem the drift toward a man-centered approach to theology? We would be wise to set aside the new reformation and return to the old one. Let's not shrink from preaching the unpopular doctrines of Paul—the total depravity of man and the spiritual deadness of the unconverted. Of course, we should preach in love and without self-righteous judgmentalism. But truth is truth, and half-truths often do the same damage as error.

Please don't interpret this position to mean that we must angrily denounce sin from a pedestal of self-righteousness. Far too many angry pastors vent their hostility by railing against sin as if they themselves do not participate in the pollution of the human race. We must preach biblical messages but in a spirit of personal repentance and humility.

We should not blush to admit with Luther and Calvin that repentance is a gift of God, granted to those who cast themselves on His mercy. The worship of God is man's highest calling. Indeed, creation exists for His good pleasure. This traditional emphasis leads us to self-understanding. Far from stripping us of dignity, such exaltation of God would help us to see ourselves as He sees us.

King Nebuchadnezzar saw himself as Christian humanists would recommend today: he had self-confidence, esteem, and, apparently, an integrated personality. He was a positive thinker whose great plans were realized. "Is this not Babylon the great, which I myself have built as a royal residence by the might of my power and for the glory of my majesty?" he asked (Dan. 4:30 NASB). His hunger for glory was satisfied.

God's response was to smite him with insanity. Nebuchadnezzar lived with the beasts of the field and ate grass like the cattle. His hair grew like eagles' feathers and his nails like birds' claws. That experience delivered him from a distorted view of himself. When he finally saw himself as he was before God, his sanity and position as king were restored.

He then blessed God and offered this praise:

For His dominion is an everlasting dominion,
And His kingdom endures from generation to generation.
And all the inhabitants of the earth are accounted as nothing,
But He does according to His will in the host of heaven
And among the inhabitants of earth;
And no one can ward off His hand
or say to Him, "What hast Thou done?"
(Dan. 4:34–35 NASB)

Thereafter, God blessed him, because he knew that he was the clay and God was the Potter. Nebuchadnezzar understood that God came first in theology. In our slide toward narcissistic preoccupation with ourselves rather than God, this is a truth we need to reaffirm.

# Priorities

---

## *How Can I Get My Act Together?*

No pastor wants to climb the ladder of success only to discover that his ladder was leaning against the wrong wall!

We all want to end with the satisfaction of knowing that we have done not just good things but the best things. In serving Christ, Martha did what was *beneficial*, but Jesus pointed out that she had neglected the one thing that was *needful*. Despite her good intentions, she had a problem with priorities.

Success is a series of right choices. Each day we stand at a fork in the road. When we say yes to one activity, we must say no to another. A night out with the family means we disappoint the hospital patient who thinks a visit from the pastor is overdue. Saying yes to a luncheon means less time for study.

"Effective leadership," Ted Engstrom says, "is the willingness to sacrifice for the sake of predetermined objectives." We've got to know what we want to achieve and then go for it with single-minded determination. As D. L. Moody said, "This one thing do . . . , not these forty things I dabble in."

But what should our priorities be? How should our time be spent when there is an endless array of good things from which we must choose? The thought that we are going to have to give an account to Christ "for the deeds done in the body, whether good or bad," should sober us and help us get our priorities straight.

Each pastor has to determine the specifics for himself. There is no one right answer to the question of how much time to spend each week in counseling versus visitation. Those matters will be determined by your gifts, the size of your church, and the expectations of your congregation. But principles exist that should guide us regardless of our specific job descriptions. The following list of priorities helps me sort out the many options that confront all of us in ministry.

## Praying Is More Important Than Preaching

When I say that "praying is more important than preaching," I don't mean we must give more time to prayer than to study—though there might be times when that would be profitable. What I mean is that we must guard our time for prayer even more closely than our time for study. When we're forced to choose, prayer should get top priority.

That was true of Christ, who spent a large part of His ministry in prayer. One day, His miracles so astonished the crowd that the whole city gathered at the door. It was a pastor's dream; people were everywhere. The next morning, He arose early and went to a secluded place to pray. Peter and some of the other disciples interrupted Him, saying, "Everyone is looking for You" (Mark 1:37 NASB).

What would we have done? We'd have returned to Capernaum to meet the expectations of the crowd. But Christ said to His disciples, "Let us go somewhere else—to the nearby villages—so I can preach there also. That is why I have come" (v. 38 NIV).

Because He had other responsibilities, He left the multitude disappointed. He refused to let the crowd dictate His schedule. Prayer in the morning hours was more important than ministry.

Jesus taught that men ought always to pray and not to faint, implying that we will do one or the other. Though a man of God may be naturally gifted, he must develop through travail in prayer. E. M. Bounds was right when he said, "Prayer that carries heaven by storm and moves God by a restless advocacy makes the pulpit a throne and its deliverances like the decrees of destiny."

Though we ought to spend much time preparing our minds for preaching, great men of the past have often spent the same amount of time in prayer, preparing their souls. Prayer, it is said, is not the preparation for the work, *it is* the work.

If your prayer life is mediocre or inconsistent, your first priority is to set aside time for this exercise. It doesn't have to be in the morning, but I've learned that if I do not spend time with God before 9:00 in the morning, I might not pray for the rest of the day. You might want to begin with fifteen minutes or half an hour. But whatever you do, make it such a priority that only an emergency would make you miss your appointment with God in prayer.

## Preaching Is More Important Than Administration

Many pastors spend so much time running the church that they have little time for study and reflection. The temptation is to spend most of our time in our "comfort zones." The one who enjoys study often ignores administration; the one who thrives on administration tends to neglect study. Blessed is the church whose pastor has both gifts.

Committees are necessary. Even more important is vision and the ability to move the congregation toward the goals of the church. But when push comes to shove, it's the ministry of the Word that gives us our greatest impact. A church can usually put up with weak administration if it has effective preaching. But there's nothing quite as pathetic as people coming to a church and returning home without spiritual food.

One way to carve more time out of a busy day is to exercise the art of delegation. Ask yourself what you are doing that someone else could do; be generous in giving away all the responsibilities you reasonably can. Doing so will save you several hours per week. Have we forgotten that no one person has all the gifts, that the Lord has places for others in the body? Or are we so desirous to maintain control that we will let nothing go from our hands? Perhaps our desire for control is best left at the foot of the cross.

The wise pastor will concentrate on his strengths and delegate other responsibilities. Personally, I prefer to say no to invitations to serve on other boards, committees, and meetings to which I am invited. Since my primary gifts are preaching and writing, I want to use them to the best of my ability.

Join me in making this resolution: that *we make preaching our one big business.*

## The Family Is More Important Than the Congregation

The importance of the family has been stressed so often that it scarcely needs to be mentioned. But many of us still have not gotten the message. As pastors, we receive our affirmation from the congregation; our successes or failures are known by many people, not by just a handful in an office. As a result, we feel vulnerable to the pressure of public opinion. This explains the strong temptation to meet the expectations of our congregations above the needs of our wives and children.

The pastor often feels as if he has many bosses. But keeping all of them happy will drive him to ignore the feelings of those he loves dearly—those who will, at least for a time, put up with neglect.

To reinforce our conviction that the family is more important than the congregation, each of us ought to make some hard, deliberate choices in our families' favor. We should take our wives and children out for ice cream rather than attend a finance committee meeting— at least once! Spend an evening on a family project rather than attend the meeting of the Sunday school council.

As I look back over my years of ministry, I wish I had been more relaxed, more spontaneous with my wife and children. I've tried to cut down on outside speaking engagements for the benefit of my family and the church. But often it's those small daily decisions that really reveal whether we value our families above those who pay our salaries.

Start today by making some tough choices in favor of your family. Let's not be easily seduced by the wide spread notion that "quality time" will make up for the quantity. There has to be a balance, of course, but usually it is our families who come up short.

## Faithfulness Is More Important Than Competition

It's easy to get discouraged in the ministry when we compare ourselves with others. Members of our congregation compare us with television preachers or the superchurch pastor who is in his third building program.

Stories of successful ministries are legion. If we focus on them, we will soon be dissatisfied with our acre in the Lord's vineyard. We know we have overcome a spirit of comparison when we are able to rejoice in the success of those who are more gifted than we are. When we are content with our little part in the total work of God on earth, we will have a sense of satisfaction and fulfillment.

A legend states that one day Christ asked each of His disciples to pick up a stone and carry it. Then, after a few days, He turned the stones into bread. Those who had chosen larger stones were glad they did. When Christ asked them to choose stones again, all the disciples chose heavy ones. But after many days, Christ had them simply throw the stones into the river. The disciples were bewildered, wondering at the purposelessness of it all. But Christ said to them, "For whom do you carry the stones?"

If we carry the stones for Christ, what He does with them will not make any difference. The issue is not whether our stones become bread but whether our Master is pleased. Faithfulness, not success as generally defined, is what He seeks.

## Love Is More Important Than Ability

Obviously, we cannot function without gifts that qualify us for the demands of the ministry. We must know the Word and be able to communicate it. And we must have skills in leadership and working with people.

Yet, surprisingly, Paul gave those essentials a lesser place than the quality of our love. Speaking with impressive ability, exercising the gift of prophecy, having the faith to move mountains, and even giving all possessions to the poor—all these actions, without love, are folly (1 Cor. 13:1–3).

Of course, love in itself would not qualify us to shepherd a congregation. But Paul would tell us we ought to concentrate on love first. When faced with a choice, we ought to develop the ability to love rather than the ability to minister.

Even the best Bible teaching does not change lives if it's not filtered through a personality filled with love. When we preach against sin harshly, we seldom motivate the congregation to godliness. But when we preach with brokenness and love, the Holy Spirit melts hardened hearts. We cannot say it often enough: *Without love, we are nothing.*

For many of us, more than half of our ministry is over. We will never pass this way again. If our priorities are misplaced, now is the time to get our house in order. Before we know it, our ministries will be over.

Look over your week's schedule and ask what you would change if you lived it according to God's priorities. When a famous sculptor was asked how he made an elephant, he answered, "I take a block of marble and cut out everything that doesn't look like elephant."
Take that block of time and cut out everything that isn't a top priority. List your activities based on comparative worth. By deliberately choosing to give more time to those things God thinks are important, we will probably find that we are accomplishing as much as ever. When we seek first the kingdom of God and His righteousness, our productivity does not cease. Only when we have done what is essential do we give God an opportunity to add to our ministries other matters that formerly were our primary concern.

If our priorities aren't straight, our ministries won't be either.

# • 18 •

# Failure

*Why Does It Sometimes Happen?*

Recently, I spoke to a discouraged pastor. His deacons were not supporting him, the congregation was apathetic, and his wife was complaining about his salary.

He was searching for an honorable exit, a way to resign with dignity. He planned to apply as a salesman with a firm that he had worked with before seminary.

Regardless of whether he had been called to the ministry, he felt as if he had given it his best but in return was greeted with one discouraging experience after another.

## What Constitutes Failure?

Was that pastor a failure? The answer depends on one's perspective.

There are at least two kinds of failure. We can fail in the eyes of men. That hurts our egos. Those of us in public ministries are observed by many people; there's no such thing as resigning "quietly." And unless we move to larger churches, we're often viewed as failures.

Of course, it's possible to fail in the eyes of men and succeed in the eyes of God. The prophet Isaiah was called to be a failure (Isa. 6). If you measured his ministry by statistics, he would not win the Most Outstanding Prophet award.

But the reverse is also possible: we can succeed in the eyes of men and yet fail in the sight of God. In this second kind of failure, we may tell ourselves that our success is for the glory of God, but the hidden motive may still be self-aggrandizement.

This leads to a question: Is it possible to be called by God and yet fail in our calling? Yes. That's what happened to the disciples in Luke 9.

## The Failure of the Disciples

Peter, James, and John had just come down from the Mount of Transfiguration with the Lord Jesus Christ. A crowd of people had gathered to watch the disciples free a boy from demonic enslavement.

The boy's father ran toward Christ, shouting, "Teacher, I beg You to look at my son, for he is my only boy, and behold, a spirit seizes him, and he suddenly screams, and it throws him into a convulsion with foaming at the mouth, and as it mauls him, it scarcely leaves him. And I begged Your disciples to cast it out, and they could not" (Luke 9:38–40 NASB).

*And they could not!* There you have failure in the ministry. As any preacher knows, it's tough to get a crowd; when you've got one, you'd like to be at your best. But though the disciples wanted to see God glorified, they couldn't perform the miracle. The crowd was about to leave disappointed.

Let's give the disciples credit for trying. Some pastors would never even attempt to cast out a demon. At least the disciples exposed themselves to the possibility of failure. They did not back off.

Yet they failed. Did they go beyond their calling? Were they attempting a task that was beyond their ability and depth? No. Earlier, Christ had called the Twelve, and He "gave them power and authority over *all* the demons" (Luke 9:1 NASB, emphasis added). They should have been able to cast out this disobedient demon.

Were they out of the will of God? No, they were exactly where God wanted them. But sometimes, while doing the will of God, we experience some of the greatest difficulties we have ever experienced. We can fail at the very task to which God calls us.

On an earlier occasion, the disciples were asked to go across the Sea of Galilee and meet Christ on the other side. Yet, even as they obeyed, they encountered one of the greatest storms on the lake. Yes, the will of God is often fraught with difficulty and danger; it is often the very place we experience the most resistance.

But now, as the disciples stood at the base of this mountain trying to cast out a demon, their call seemed ineffective, their commission

wasn't successful, and their authority didn't work. Why? Three reasons come from the text.

### Reasons for Their Failure

First, they lacked *faith*. Christ answers them, "O unbelieving and
perverted generation, how long shall I be with you, and put up with
you?" (v. 41).

Christ calls them unbelieving. Whatever the cause, they didn't
have faith for this particular miracle.

We as pastors can identify. Almost every problem in the congregation eventually comes to our attention. We see divorce, moral failure,
and personality conflicts. Under the weight of such discouragements,
it's easy to entertain doubt.

"If Christ's power is so great, why doesn't He heal this marriage?
Why doesn't He . . . ?" At that point, we're on the verge of being spiritually paralyzed, unable to fulfill our calling. Without faith, we are
powerless.

We know how discouraging it can be when nothing goes as planned,
when our family is being attacked by Satan, and when church members
turn against us. When our confidence in God is eroded, we are vulnerable to failure. Christ called His disciples an "unbelieving generation."

Second, they lacked *discipline*. In the parallel passage in Matthew 17,
the disciples asked Christ why they could not cast out the demon,
and He replied, "Because of the littleness of your faith; for truly I say
to you, if you have faith as a mustard seed, you shall say to this
mountain, 'Move from here to there,' and it shall move; and nothing
shall be impossible to you" (Matt. 17:20 NASB). Then Christ added,
"But this kind does not go out except by prayer and fasting" (v. 21).

Prayer and fasting! The disciples' authority was not automatic.
Just because they had cast out demons in the past did not mean they
could count on such authority in the future. Their calling would have
to be renewed by fervent prayer and fasting.

Maybe they were too busy for a time of spiritual refreshment. They
may have begun to live off their own success stories and to think
they were too busy for the basics.

We're not very adept at fasting. Warren Wiersbe says, "Call a feast
and everyone is there. Call a fast and nobody shows." Without discipline, our ability to function spiritually is jeopardized.

There is a story about a man who was chopping trees, flailing away, the sweat running down his brow. A friend stopped by and asked whether he had sharpened his ax. The answer: "No, I have to get these trees down by noon, so I don't have time to sharpen my ax." But of course, we all know that the ten minutes needed to sharpen his ax would have been well spent. Similarly, the spiritual disciplines are the means by which we are refreshed, our ax is sharpened.

Third, they lacked *humility*. They asked a question we hear repeatedly in our day: "Who is the greatest in the kingdom of heaven?" (Luke 9:46). Who has the greatest church, the greatest Sunday school? Who is the greatest preacher, the greatest author?

Those questions reveal a carnal sense of comparison. On a dark night, we can argue about which star is the brightest, but when the sun comes out it makes no difference—all stars fade in its brightness.

Paul said that those who "compare themselves with themselves" are "without understanding" (2 Cor. 10:12). We don't know who the greatest preacher is. That's for God to judge. When we stop comparing ourselves with ourselves and compare ourselves with Christ, we find that there isn't much difference between us.

The disciples' pride led to a spirit of criticism also. They tried to prevent someone else from casting out demons in the name of Christ "because he does not follow along with us" (Luke 9:49 NASB). This person was successful in the very ministry in which they had failed. Like us, they tended to be suspicious of those who were succeeding at a task in which they were floundering.

God often uses people who don't agree with me. My pride has occasionally prevented me from rejoicing in the success of those who don't belong to my denomination or who differ from my theology. When we are humble, we will rejoice in the success of others and we will give God the credit for whatever little success we might have.

Do you remember the story in the book of Acts when the sons of Sceva tried to cast out a demon in the name of Jesus? They had watched Paul deliver people in the name of Jesus, so these young men thought they could do the same. They thought the name of Jesus was a good luck charm that could be used whenever they wished. But they were in for a surprise.

"And the evil spirit answered and said to them, 'I recognize Jesus, and I know about Paul, but who are you?' And the man, in whom was the evil spirit, leaped on them and subdued both of them and over-powered them, so that they fled out of that house naked and wounded" (Acts 19:15–16 NASB).

The lesson? We cannot take our authority for granted. There is more to winning against Satan than simply using the name of Jesus. Without devotion and discipline, we will discover that we cannot do ministry.

## Reasons for Our Failure

Today, people still gather to see a display of Christ's power. They want to see drug addicts converted and marriages saved. They want to hear songs sung with joy and the Word preached with power. But unless we have faith, discipline, and humility, we will not be able to fulfill our calling.

We'll say to this mountain, "Be cast into the sea," or we will command the demon, "Be gone in Jesus' name." Neither will budge, and the crowds will leave disappointed. We know we were called, but our authority has evaporated. We've failed in God's work.

Maybe my pastor friend who is planning to become a salesman wasn't called to be a pastor. Or maybe he's in the wrong church. Then again, he might be in the will of God but passing through a desert experience. He just needs someone to encourage him, to let him know that he is appreciated. Or perhaps he has taken his calling for granted and has begun to live off substitutes. It may be that he has lost his authority, not his calling. That's why the mountains aren't moving and the demons refuse to leave.

I've learned that when I cannot exercise my authority to minister, God is calling me back to the basics. Faith, discipline, and humility can restore us to the place of blessing. Even commissioned disciples fail when they take their calling for granted.

## • 19 •

# The Fallen

## *How Can We Reach Out and Restore?*

A seminary professor once told his students that they should become familiar with a vocation other than preaching because a certain percentage of them would eventually fall into immorality and have to leave the ministry. Although we might cringe at such advice, the professor was probably right.

A few months ago when I heard that a friend had to resign because of adultery, my reaction was, "He's the last person I'd expect that to happen to." But, unfortunately, the last is often the first.

### The High Price of Sin

Recently, I asked some evangelical leaders whether a man who had fallen into sexual immorality should be restored to the pastorate. They said it's possible but highly unlikely. According to 1 Timothy 3:2, an elder is to be "blameless" (KJV) or "above reproach" (NASB). It's difficult to regain the public trust and to rebuild a reputation destroyed on the rocks of infidelity.

Many people believe, however, that Paul's standards in that passage refer to the *present* spiritual condition of an elder. For example, he is to be "free from the love of money" (v. 3), but that doesn't rule out the possibility that he did love money even after he was converted. There is growth in the Christian life; there is change and transformation.

These qualities refer to a man who has moved on spiritually and put his past life of sin behind him. At first glance, it seems reasonable that if a man falls into sexual sin, repents, and submits himself to the discipline of his church, he could once again be "blameless," because he has dealt with his sin biblically.

With that in mind, I asked the same leaders if their church or denomination would ever call as a pastor a man who had fallen but over time had demonstrated the fruits of repentance. Again, they answered no, unless many years had elapsed and the matter was long forgotten. Some of them knew of cases, however, in which a man was restored to an effective pulpit ministry, but his congregation did not know about his past.

My informal survey, however, was conducted several years before some rather high-profile pastors who had fallen into sexual sin were restored. I suspect that if the same questions were asked today, many leaders would be more open to the possibility of restoration to ministry. I can rejoice in such restoration, but I am also concerned that the high standards for ministry are being eroded. What does such restoration to the pulpit say to young men who are tempted to find fulfillment outside of their own marriage bond? Knowing that the mind can rationalize any sin that the heart wants to do, it is easy for a minister to think, "Look at so-and-so. He sinned and yet was restored. That's not so bad."

Marshall Shelley writes, "On the one hand, pastors are full-fledged members of the human race. They sin daily. On the other hand, pastors labor in a profession in which character is critical. They're called to lead and teach and model not some technical skill, but a life. When pastors fall, they can wound many believers."[1]

Yes, it is impossible for a pastor to stumble without causing others to be hindered in the race of life. Some will be emboldened to sin; others will lose confidence that sexual purity can be preserved.

An argument could be made that we are inconsistent in our standards. While sexual sin has routinely required stepping down from the ministry, sins of the spirit have been overlooked. The apostle John defined three root sins: pride, covetousness, and lust (1 John 2:16). Yet, I have never known of a pastor who had to resign because of pride or the love of money.

Martin Luther wrote, "God frequently permits a man to fall into or remain in grievous sin so that he may be put to shame in his own eyes and in the eyes of all men. Otherwise, he could not have kept himself free of this great vice of vain honor and a famous name if he had remained constant in his great gifts and virtues."[2] Yes, often pride lies at the root of other sins, even sexual immorality.

But regardless of how offensive pride is to God, sexual sin is in a class by itself. Paul wrote, "Flee immorality. Every other sin that a man commits is outside the body, but the immoral man sins against his own body" (1 Cor. 6:18 NASB).

Sexuality is such an intimate part of our lives, we cannot fail in it without guilt and shame. In adultery, there is also the constant reminder of the consequences of sin in someone else's life. What is more, the marriage relationship is to mirror Christ and His church. When a pastor shatters the intimate bond of marriage, we should think that he forfeited his right to the pulpit.

Sexual sin is usually accompanied by other sins. A person who commits adultery breaks at least five of the Ten Commandments. He puts his desires above God, steals, covets, bears false witness, and breaks the explicit commandment "You shall not commit adultery" (Exod. 20:14 NASB).

John Armstrong, in his helpful book *Can Fallen Pastors Be Restored?* writes, "Thus when we commit sexual sins we transgress directly against God's ordered plan for creation and His awesome holiness. We aggressively attack His holy name, His holy character and His holy law."[3] The breaking of a marriage vow, the violation of another person in an intimate unholy union, and the destroying of the picture of trust between Christ and the Church—this is a serious matter indeed.

Because of the shame of sexual sin, there is an overwhelming tendency to commit other sins to cover the deed. If someone had told King David he would get a man drunk and eventually have him murdered, he wouldn't have believed it. Yet, sexual sin made him a liar, a thief, and a murderer.

One denominational leader who had investigated a number of instances of alleged infidelity said he was surprised at how often pastors would lie, even invoking God's name, in covering their sin. Yet, we shouldn't be surprised. If a man can violate one of God's clearest commandments, other sins come easily.

A person who falls into this sin also tends to develop a pattern of infidelity. One pastor's wife complained that her husband was unfaithful not only in their first church but also in each successive pastorate. He kept believing he could get by because no one was willing to blow the whistle.

Sexual sin is a serious offense. Nevertheless, too often we force a man to the sidelines because of a single immoral act that we refuse to forgive and forget. Some former pastors have genuinely repented and have accepted the discipline of the church. Even if they cannot be restored to the pastorate, they could be used effectively in related ministries.

## The Possibility of Restoration

In Galatians 6:1, Paul answers the questions we might have about restoration: "Brethren, even if a man is caught in any trespass, you who are spiritual, restore such a one in a spirit of gentleness; looking to yourselves, lest you too be tempted" (NASB).

What does it mean to restore one who has fallen? The Greek word *katartizo* was also used to refer to setting a broken bone. Unfortunately, many bones in the body of Christ have remained out of joint and have never been restored.

In a typical case of a pastor who commits grievous sin, he resigns almost immediately, has nowhere to go, and is forced to leave the area. Often, his salary is cut off with no provision made for his future. Because of his shame, he does not seek the fellowship of his friends. They feel awkward about approaching him, so a curtain of silence falls around him and his family.

The minister's wife is usually much more deeply wounded than she can ever tell. Committed as she is to Christ and the church, she must say all the right words, that yes, she forgives her husband, and yes, she will make the marriage work. But it might take years for the trust to be rebuilt and the joy to return to their relationship. She has to live with the painful reality that her husband violated their personal covenant and shared sexual intimacy with someone else. No wonder the restoration of their marriage takes time. This is a process that cannot be hurried along.

The couple feels ostracized, but their friends see their hasty exit as evidence that they are really not willing to be restored or repentant. The friends feel too uncomfortable to visit the wounded couple, not knowing what kind of a response they will receive or what they will say. Thus, the friendships that are so desperately needed often do not develop.

One evening, I had dinner with two friends, both of whom had to leave the ministry because of sexual sin. I asked one of them how many people had come to minister to him and how frequently his friends stopped by to pray with him. I was shocked to hear him reply, "I receive no visits; no one comes by to pray with us." That was the response even though members of the church lived close by. If we do not shoot our wounded, we most assuredly leave them bleeding along the side of the road.

Paul identified who should take the initiative: "you who are spiritual." When someone falls into sin, the difference between carnal Christians and spiritual Christians becomes clear. Under the guise of holiness, carnal believers will be critical, always demanding the maximum penalty.

One denominational leader told me that when a brother falls, some people almost show delight rather than sorrow and remorse. The self-righteous believer uses the opportunity for self-exaltation, seeming to enjoy picking on a brother who has been wounded. No matter how many sins are in his own life, a self-righteous man will see a pastor's moral failure as one more reason either to justify his own indiscretions or to make himself feel a tad more righteous.

A group of pastors sat discussing the news that a fellow minister had resigned amid rumors of sexual unfaithfulness. Yet, when one of them asked whether anyone had contacted him, they were reduced to silence. No one had.

The truly spiritual believer will be grieved and ask how his comrade can be restored. It's not the fallen brother who should do the restoring; the initiative should come from sensitive, spiritual Christians. They will be willing to risk reaching out despite the possibility of being misunderstood and accused of being "soft on sin."

Finally, how should restoration be done? Paul said, ". . . in the spirit of meekness" (Gal. 6:1 KJV). If a person has a broken bone, he doesn't want it pushed into place with a crowbar. It needs to be set with gentleness. There is no room for condemnation or self-righteousness. We must be aware that we could commit the same sin.

If the brother acknowledges his sin and repents, then fellowship can be restored. That's the first step in the long healing process.

But there is a difference between restoration to the body of Christ and restoration to ministry. Certainly, such a one will be able to serve the Lord again, though perhaps in a different capacity. We cannot predict what God might yet do through the life of a repentant, restored sinner. Sometimes the bird with the broken wing does soar again.

Let's not concede the whole tournament just because the devil has won a game.

# • 20 •

# The Church

## *What Is Christ's Blueprint?*

Whenever I'm asked, "Where is your church?" I'm tempted to answer, "On Sunday, it's at 1609 N. LaSalle Street in Chicago, but during the week, it is scattered throughout the entire Chicago area!"

The word *church* is never used in the New Testament to refer to a building but rather to the people of God, those who are "called out" by God to form the body of Christ. It refers to saints on earth as well as saints in heaven. Those churches on hilltops with cemeteries around them are communicating a powerful theological lesson: the saints militant and the saints triumphant are all part of the same family. That's why the cemetery surrounds the church—you have to walk past the alumni association before you get to the undergraduates!

I think it was Reinhold Niebuhr who wrote that the church reminded him of Noah's ark—you couldn't take the stench within if it wasn't for the storm without! Whatever we may say about the church, this much is certain: it represents the highest priority on God's agenda and is His blueprint for completing His plans on earth. When Christ predicted the formation of the church, He highlighted certain features to which we must return again and again if we don't want to waste our time taking costly detours. His words are familiar: "And I also say to you that you are Peter, and upon this rock I will build My church; and the gates of Hades will not overpower it" (Matt. 16:18 NASB).

If we understand the features of the church, we will be able to serve with freedom and joy. What do we learn about the church in this statement?

## Christ Owns the Church

"I will build My church." Believers were purchased at high cost; understandably, we are God's property. If the value of an object is determined by the price paid for it, then we are valuable indeed. We are not purchased with silver and gold but with the costly blood of Christ. The cross of Christ is an everlasting testimony to how much believers are actually worth to God! Of course, we are not valuable in and of ourselves; we are valuable because He chose to love us. In choosing to die for us, our Lord affirmed that we are infinitely precious to Him.

The implications for our ministry are obvious. God's people do not exist for their own benefit but for *His* benefit. In our interpersonal relationships, we must remember that we are dealing with God's property, His people redeemed for His own purposes. That's why church leaders are exhorted to humility and not to dictatorial leadership: "Therefore, I exhort the elders among you, as your fellow-elder . . . , shepherd the flock of God among you, not under compulsion, but voluntarily, according to the will of God; and not for sordid gain, but with eagerness; nor yet as lording it over those allotted to your charge, but proving to be examples to the flock" (1 Peter 5:1–3 NASB).

There's no place for manipulation or coercion within the church. Certainly, church leaders have to exercise authority as the Scriptures teach but not with the hidden motive of making their ministries appear successful. All fund-raising techniques and building programs must be examined closely; hidden motives must continually come under the scrutiny of God's microscope. Why? Because we are dealing with His people, His handiwork.

Furthermore, we are accountable to one another. The leader who says, "I am accountable only to God," speaks arrogantly and ignorantly. He forgets that God expects mutual submission and servanthood from every member of the body. All believers belong to the same family and have privileges and responsibilities.

Whenever I use carnal methods to accomplish worthy goals, I have forgotten who owns the church; whenever I am envious of those who are more successful than I am or whenever I use the church to exalt my abilities or to give the appearance of success, I have forgotten who owns the church.

What a relief to realize that the people in my congregation are God's property! Aren't you glad that those who stubbornly refuse to see your viewpoint don't belong to you? Like Moses, we must tell God from time to time, "Remember, these are Your people!"

If you have never given your congregation to God, do so right now. You will find a new freedom to serve when you recognize God as the rightful owner of His people.

Now, for a second feature of the church.

## Christ Builds the Church

"I will build My church," Christ said. In all of our discipleship and evangelism, we must realize that we cannot do Christ's work for Him. Before He left, He gave instructions to the disciples to "make disciples of all nations" just as He had done while He was on earth. Now we are His representatives, standing in for Him during this period of His physical absence from earth. He did not make disciples en masse, nor can we!

Several years ago, I attended a joint session of the National Religious Broadcasters and the National Association of Evangelicals in Washington, D.C. Hundreds of displays exhibited the latest in technology, all used to spread the gospel around the world. After walking through acres of equipment, I began to wonder how the early church ever made it!

They, of course, made disciples the hard way, one person pouring his life into another in "on-the-job" training. Since those believers could not rely on the mass media, they felt an obligation to witness with their own lives and lips to everyone who crossed their paths. That's how the church was built, and that's how Christ intends that it be built today. We can be grateful for the Christian mass media, but there is no shortcut to building the church.

The stones for Solomon's temple were cut in a distant quarry and then brought into the temple area and assembled without the noise of a hammer. In Ephesians, Paul says that God is building a habitation, and believers are the stones. He chooses those whom He will save and brings them into a relationship with both one another and Himself. He fits us into the building as it pleases Him. He is building a place in which He Himself will dwell (Eph. 2:20–22).

Building the church is not left up to us, though we participate in the process. Our responsibility is to find how Christ did it and then reproduce His methods. Recognizing that He is the primary builder gives us hope and courage in the building process.

Today, much is written about church growth methodology and how to make a church more appealing to "seekers." Certainly, there is much we can learn from those who have been successful in seeing a church go from a few hundred to many thousands. The problem is that the success is often explained in terms of this particular method or that particular approach. Isn't it time that we saw churches grow with no explanation except that Christ has sovereignly chosen to build His church?

How refreshing it is to find a church whose only explanation is prayer, worship, and sensitivity to the leading of the Holy Spirit! Of course, I do not mean that we should expect a church to grow without training in evangelism, missions, and disciple making. He uses us to do His work. We have to plan, strategize, and determine what God wants us to do. Paul says that "we labor together with Christ." But in the end, our people should be convinced that what they have seen is the hand of the Almighty.

Christ is often robbed of the credit He so richly deserves whenever we try to find human explanations for a divine enterprise. Let us learn what we can from the experts, but let us never point to methods as an explanation for success. We must intentionally depend on Him for the growth of the church and make sure that He gets the praise when it happens.

One further implication: If a particular church is not growing numerically, it might not always be the fault of Christ's human instruments. Churches in hostile countries have sometimes been diminished through persecution and cultural conflicts. Even in our own country, there are times when the church itself is not at fault if it is not growing numerically. I say that not to excuse sloth and lack of vision, but simply to affirm that the growth of the church ultimately rests with Christ and not with us. And yet there is more.

## Christ Preserves the Church

"The gates of Hades will not overpower it," Christ said (Matt. 16:18 NASB). This expression probably refers to His impending death. The same description is used by Hezekiah in Isaiah 38:10 to refer to his own death. What Christ seems to be saying is this: Although the gates of Hades will close behind Me, they are powerless to keep Me within their grasp. The advance of the church will not be halted by such apparent setbacks. The church is indestructible.

That ought to take some of the pressure off our schedules! We can be involved in building the church with a sense of trust, believing that God's ultimate purposes will be accomplished. When the believers in Rome saw the unbelief of Israel as frustrating the purpose of God, Paul assured them, "But it is not as though the word of God has failed. For they are not all Israel who are descended from Israel" (Rom. 9:6 NASB).

The imagery is that of a ship that has not drifted from its intended destination. Paul is saying that the word of God is not "off course." God's purposes are on schedule; His work in the world continues, and it will be accomplished.

Paul writes in Ephesians 2:20–22, "Having been built upon the foundation of the apostles and prophets, Christ Jesus Himself being the corner stone, in whom the whole building, being fitted together is growing into a holy temple in the Lord; in whom you also are being built together into a dwelling of God in the Spirit" (NASB).

Notice the three passive verbs that Paul uses to show that the church is both built and preserved by God. We, "having been built," are also "being fitted" and again are "being built together into a dwelling of God in the Spirit." Believers are being acted upon by God, who is in the process of doing His work on earth. Like the stones referred to earlier, God is using His chisel and hammer to ready the church for His own purposes.

What an encouragement! To be involved with Christ in the building of the church is a no-risk venture. Eventual success is guaranteed. Peter Marshall said, "It is better to fail in a cause that will eventually succeed than to succeed in a cause that will eventually fail." Think about the implications: though we may fail in many ways, we are embarked upon an enterprise that has God's highest priority, and eventual success is inevitable. The gates of Hades will not prevail against it.

## Christ Empowers the Church

To Peter Christ said, "I will give you the keys of the kingdom of heaven; and whatever you shall bind on earth shall have been bound in heaven, and whatever you shall loose on earth shall have been loosed in heaven" (Matt. 16:19 NASB). Later, Christ gave the same authority to all the apostles.

Here, Christ is giving the apostles power to carry out their assignment. It's unthinkable that He would give the disciples a blueprint and not give them the ability to carry it out. If I send my child to the store to get some groceries, I must give her the money to buy the items. Whether the list is long or short, whether it is costly or cheap, she must look to me for the resources to pay. Christ must give resources to those who would work with Him in building the church. Because all authority has been given to Him, He can say to us, "Go ye therefore."

The church is God's number one priority in the world. It displays His wisdom, both now and in the ages to come, "in order that the manifold wisdom of God might now be made known through the church to the rulers and the authorities in the heavenly places. This was in accordance with the eternal purpose which He carried out in Jesus Christ our Lord" (Eph. 3:10–11 NASB).

Christ has not left us alone. He resides in us and works with us in the building of His church. When Augustine was told that Rome had been sacked, he reportedly said, "Whatever men build, men will destroy . . . , so let's get on with building the kingdom of God."

Since whatever men build, men will destroy, let us get on with the business of building the church, for our Lord has promised that the gates of Hades cannot prevail against it. No risk is entailed. We have His promise of eternal success.

# Notes

## Chapter 1
1. Garry Friesen, *Decision Making and the Will of God* (Portland, Oreg.: Multnomah, 1981).
2. J. Oswald Sanders, *Spiritual Leadership* (Chicago: Moody Press, 1994), 18.
3. John Jowett, *The Preacher: His Life and Work* (Grand Rapids: Baker, 1968), 21.
4. Ibid., 12.

## Chapter 3
1. Bruce Stabbert, *The Team Concept* (Tacoma, Wash.: Hegg Brothers, 1982).

## Chapter 4
1. Marshall Shelley, *Well-Intentioned Dragons* (Carol Stream, Ill.: Christianity Today, 1985), 110.
2. Ibid., 107.
3. Ibid., 133.

## Chapter 5
1. John Owen, *Sin and Temptation* (Portland, Oreg.: Multnomah, 1983), xviii.

## Chapter 10
1. J. Grant Swank Jr., "Who Counsels Pastors When They Have Problems?" *Christianity Today,* 25 November 1983, 58.
2. David Congo, *Theology News and Notes* (March 1984): 8.

3. Iain Murray, *Jonathon Edwards* (Scotland: Banner of Truth Trust, 1987), 327.
4. James B. Scott, *Theology News and Notes* (March 1984): 15.

**Chapter 11**
1. Francis Schaeffer, *The Great Evangelical Disaster* (Westchester, Ill.: Crossway, 1984), 37.

**Chapter 12**
1. Lawrence Crabb, *Effective Biblical Counseling* (Grand Rapids: Zondervan, 1977), 47.

**Chapter 13**
1. William Temple, quoted in John MacArthur, *The Ultimate Priority* (Chicago: Moody Press, 1983), 147.
2. Ibid., 104.
3. John Stott, *Between Two Worlds* (Grand Rapids: Eerdmans, 1982), 82–83.

**Chapter 14**
1. Lewis Sperry Chafer, *True Evangelism* (Grand Rapids: Zondervan, 1919), 15.
2. Ibid., 14–15.

**Chapter 16**
1. Robert Schuller, *Self-Esteem—The New Reformation* (Dallas: Word, 1982), 26–27.
2. Ibid., 14.
3. Ibid., 127.

**Chapter 19**
1. Marshall Shelley, quoted in John Armstrong, *Can Fallen Pastors Be Restored?* (Chicago: Moody Press, 1995), 17.
2. James Atkinson, *Luther's Works: The Christian in Society I*, vol. 44 (Philadelphia: Fortress, 1966), 45.
3. Armstrong, op. cit., 51.

## Also by Erwin Lutzer

# *The Doctrines That Divide*

### *A Fresh Look at the Historic Doctrines That Separate Christians*

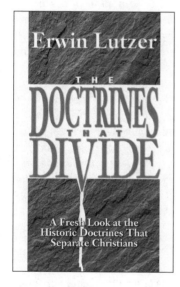

Lutzer examines various controversies that exist within the broad sprectrum of Christianity, presenting the historical background of the issue and the biblical understanding of the doctrine.

*The Doctrines That Divide* provides a non-combative look at "hot button" issues in the church, which include

- infant baptism
- the deity and humanity of Christ
- the sacraments
- the worship of Mary
- predestination or free will
- justification by faith or works
- the canon of Scripture
- eternal security
- the sovereignty of God

ISBN 0-8254-3165-4    256 pp.

*"I recommend this book highly. The writer is a patient, persuasive pastor and never resorts to name-calling or condemnation. . . . buy this book!"*

—Harold Lindsell

## Lessons in Leadership
### by Randal Roberts, general editor

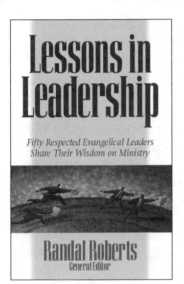

ISBN 0-8254-3630-3     288 pp.

*Dear Friend,*

*Now, you have no doubt heard the old adage that a pastor needs "the mind of a scholar, the heart of a child, and the skin of a rhinoceros," and there is a certain amount of truth therein. But I prefer to think of the pastor as a person called to be a servant of God, a proclaimer of truth, and a lover of people. And there's a bittersweetness to all three. . . .*

*Wherever I go, the people of this fellowship to whom I've devoted many years of my life smile at me, their hands reach out to me . . . [And] in some strange way they let me know that I belong in their midst and they in some indefinable manner belong in my life. No one told me that being a pastor would be like this.*

*Sincerely,*
*Stuart Briscoe*

This and forty-nine other letters offer insightful counsel for pastors or seminary students from today's Christian leaders, pastors, and professors, including

- Bill Bright
- Jill Briscoe
- Ted Engstrom
- Kenneth O. Gangel

- Carl F. H. Henry
- Walter C. Kaiser Jr.
- Jay Kesler
- Woodrow Kroll

- Aubrey Malphurs
- Luis Palau
- Earl D. Radmacher
- Moishe Rosen

PUBLICATIONS

Grand Rapids, MI  49501